Nuts and Bolts

Of a Christian Residential Program

Marilyn McDonald

Nuts and Bolts: Of a Christian Residential Program
Copyright © 2020 Marilyn McDonald
ISBN: 978-1-970153-26-2
Library of Congress:

All Proceeds go to Charity through Morning Star Church

La Maison Publishing, Inc.
Vero Beach, Florida
The Hibiscus City

Maison

You will absolutely enjoy this book and memoir of Ms. Marilyn McDonald's life's work of developing a wonderful, Christ-centered women's program, that has forever changed the lives of so many. Marilyn is a longstanding spirited, jovial member and friend of Morning Star Church ARP in Vero Beach, Florida. We are excited for her to share His story through the work of the House of Sophia. I cannot more highly recommend this book to those who are wanting to start a program like this, that brings all the Glory to Him.

-Soli Deo Gloria, Pastor Trevor Raborn, M. Div, Morning Star ARP, A Church for Vero.

In Marilyn's quest to provide a significant program for women in desperate need of help, the author envisioned, created, and put into action a unique 501(c) 3 non-profit organization. Marilyn's caring and compassionate manner, along with her great entrepreneurial spirit, saw the development of a grassroots institution that significantly improved the lives of the clients as well as the volunteers who participated. This is her story.

Bill Parkhurst, manager at YMCA for thirty years. Elder Emeritus, financial manager of the North City Church, president of House of Sophia board.

Full disclosure: I was involved in Marilyn's ministry and the writing of her book, The Nuts and Bolts of a Christian Residential Program. She mentions my work as an "advisor to the Board." Nevertheless, I also desire to commend her ministry and this volume.

As Marilyn says in the book, I was one of her teachers at Westminster Seminary in California. Marilyn came to us from a secular background, and we would not have predicted the course her life and ministry eventually took. But God did amazing things, bringing her to a deep trust in Christ as Lord and Savior, enabling her to earn a degree in biblical counseling, bringing her into a church that put her to work as a prison chaplain, and leading her to a piece of property that was well-suited to the work of "helping women." We were so thankful to God as we saw how He was changing lives through the House of Sophia. Now Marilyn has written a book that shows how her ministry can be duplicated all around the world. It is clearly written and can be an immense help to churches and Christian organizations who take up God's challenge to share Christ with needy women. Marilyn's model is not merely teaching. She presents a way by which women can put off the habits that lead them to failure and put on the Lord Jesus Christ. I hope this book gets into the hands of many churches and ministries-- anyone who seeks to help needy women to faith in the Lord and real and permanent life change.

John M. Frame
Prof. Emeritus of Systematic Theology and Philosophy
Reformed Theological Seminary, Orlando, FL

Marilyn McDonald was such a pleasure to work with during the time she cared for one of our clients. Ms. McDonald opened up her home to an adult with a developmental disability and to The AFHA, Adult Family Home Agency. She provided food, shelter, experience, love, and took on the responsibilities of training to be approved as a Family Home Provider. The impact she had on the client of 2 years showed tremendous growth in developing life skills and she formed a positive relationship with the client.

Janice Domaschenz
Psycologist Understudy

How many Christian believers want to use his/her gifts to help others but stop short of actually fulfilling this? Most do not grasp how to get started. Forming a non-profit is probably the best method, but with limited funds, it seems impossible for those who have never done this before.

Marilyn McDonald wrote this book to encourage ordinary Christians to move ahead with their dreams by sharing what she's learned over the years with her ministry to help women who had lost their way.

When I first met Marilyn, she was a student at a nearby seminary. I didn't realize she was a fairly new Christian, but I watched as she went through struggles with studies and then with fulfilling her mission through the "House of Sophia."

She grew as a Christian and has never turned back. She has been planted in the "good soil" and produced much fruit over the years. She truly loves God with all her heart and her neighbor as herself. I have been blessed by knowing her.

Nancy Houtz
Program Director of Prison Ministry, California

I have known Marilyn for over 20 years, went to seminary together and did ministry together at the House of Sophia. She is a truly remarkable person who has a lot to share with others wanting to get involved in non-profit organizations.

Rev. Jose Rayas, Valley Ridge Community Church,
Socorro, TX

I have known Marilyn since our days at Westminster Seminary in the mid-90's, when we studied together and slaved over term papers. I have watched God do a wonderful work in Marilyn's life. It has been amazing to watch Marilyn use her theological training to give hope and help to some of the most troubled women in our community, sacrificially taking them into her own home.

Deborah J. Dewart, Attorney

Acknowledgements

One of the stunning realities of the Christian life is that in the world where everything is in some state of decay, God's mercies are designed like a fountain that never stops flowing and reaches beyond the heart to grasp. The longer I live, the more people I am obliged to thank for making this book come to life. I am so grateful for how God planned for specific people to meet my own needs in establishing the House of Sophia.

Wellspring in CA., my very first church, and their Pastor Tim Spykstra, saw my vision, commissioned me as a Chaplain, and guided me to their women's ministry director who guided me in my vision for the House of Sophia. Emmanuel Faith Church in Escondido, CA followed with welcome support, and even sent me to Westminster Seminary. For a time, I was a member of New Life Church in Escondido. Later, when I moved the House of Sophia to Rancho Bernardo, CA, I was warmly welcomed and supported in the H.O.S. ministry by North City Church. Upon my retirement to Vero Beach, FL, Morning Star Church, ARP, and retired Pastor Dennis Rupert and present Pastor Trevor Raborn welcomed, and affirmed me with their own open hearts for mercy ministry. These bodies of Christ have been my nourishment and encouragement throughout my life.

My medical doctors, Dr. Sorrell, Dr. Mora, and Dr. Valeriano were among the best of physicians who blessed me throughout my ministry and kept me healthy, under the strain of difficult stressful times, including the death of my son.

Attending Westminster Seminary in California was a highlight in my life. These professors made a profound impact, transforming my life: Dr. Ian Duguid, Dr. John Frame, Dr. Mark Futato, Dr. Dennis Johnson, Dr. George Scipione, and Dr. Robert Strimple. I carry their teachings to this day. It was in Dr. Frame's class, *The Christian Mind*, that I came to trust in Jesus as my Lord and Savior.

I am grateful for three presidents on the Board of Directors: Dave Walson, a Messianic Jew, who daily prayed for me over the years and answered any questions I had about the faith; Tom Stevenson, who had the foresight as a businessman to plan my retirement to Vero Beach, FL; Bill Parkhurst, the last president, who wrote every letter that needed to be sent out. He represented me at the North City Session and was a constant source of encouragement to me. Together with his wife Barb, they have provided hospitality for years to come.

Board Members, Dick and Carmen Lafleur, were generous donors who gave wise counsel and words of encouragement when I most needed it. Carmen was the secretary and bookkeeper who gave countless hours to correspondence. Zan Stanton, whose compassionate heart for evangelistic outreach among the homeless, advanced the distribution task of food to the poor and constructed homes on the land adjacent to the H.O.S. property. Valerie Rayas, who had a master's degree and worked at the hospital, sent ladies to the H.O.S. and counseled them. Pat Vawter, a dedicated, persevering secretary who did a lot of bookwork and assisted in the modification of loans, one of them from 5% to 2%. She also continued the 501C3 now being used in Uganda, Africa. Virginia Nichols, a nutritionist, taught me how to eat right, most noteworthy, to take vitamins and replace diabetic insulin with a pill. She was a most godly, caring woman and lived to 92 years of age. Prof. John Frame, whom I mentioned among my teachers at Westminster, was an advisor to the Board, who helped me with the theology of my presentations.

Among my friends and mentors, Bill E., a servant-hearted and loyal seminary friend, wrote the House of Sophia Handbook, an overview to introduce women to the program. He served with his bookkeeping experience and could be depended upon in every way, including large donations of money. Within the body of Christ, God blessed me with special friends like Jim Newheiser, who, as the director of IBCD, supervised and counseled many of the women in the H.O.S. Jon and Sharon were wonderful friends who generously gave Creative Memory crafts, furniture and several times paid our house taxes. George (Skip) and Eileen Scipione were guides/mentors who stayed a long time at the H.O.S. and took excellent care of the ladies while I went to Africa. Other mentors and friends were Zan and Kitty Stanton, Jose and Valerie Rajas, John and Mary Frame, Nancy Houtz, Kathy Orr, Charlene Arce, Virginia Nichols, Brian, and Amanda Williams, Mitch

Briscoe, my contractor son, and Shirley Ward, my sister, who supported me every single day and pushed me to "keep going!" Debbie Dewart, also a graduate of Westminster Seminary, is a lawyer and has been very generous with her time as a precious friend to me. Debbie worked through all our legal issues at no charge. Trevor and Melissa Raborn, and Dennis Rupert, who never saw the H.O.S. in action, have understood the vision for this book. They love mercy ministry and have helped me with the final editing of these pages. By God's gracious providence, these are the people that God allowed to cross my path for friendship. They believed in the vision, embraced with support, and loved me through it — and still do! Many people are blessed if they have one or two real friends, but I have never felt as blessed as while writing these acknowledgments. I have come to realize the astounding friendships, many lasting over 20 years. As I write, I think I am recognizing that these acknowledgments have been the best part of the book because of the acute awareness of God's choosing so many to have done this program, not just me. These people came and dropped diamonds on me all the time!

My heart especially goes out to all the wonderful donors without whom the House of Sophia could not have existed. You know who you are; to God be the glory!

Dedication

I am so eternally grateful to the ladies whose stories appear in this book. May they each receive great joy from knowing that they are participating with Christ in His work of grace, to pass the hope of their new lives to the next generation for understanding and healing through Jesus Christ, the Savior of the world. I learned as much from these ladies, if not more than they learned from me in the H.O.S. as I saw their lives transformed by the power of the Holy Spirit.

Contents

Part 1

Driven by Hopelessness

Chapter 1

Lady Folly to Lady Wisdom

For I know the plans I have for you, declares the Lord, plans for welfare and not for evil, to give you a future and a hope. Jeremiah 29:11 (ESV)

Why would anyone take women addicted to substances off the streets, out of prisons, and out of traumatic life experiences into their home?

Until you walk a mile in someone else's shoes, you cannot truly know them. Before I founded the House of Sophia, I had walked 53 years as a troubled woman who had both physical and emotional abuse as a child. Later, I was diagnosed with depression and was addicted to prescription drugs. I had arrived in the business world, and my social life was luxuriant. I had everything except God, which eventually led me to seminary.

Over thirty-three years. I married twice, had two beautiful children, became a millionaire, owned two beauty salons, and founded and accredited a beauty college. I've owned multiple homes and traveled with movie stars. I had accomplished my worldly desires, and yet I felt empty and alone.

While grading papers alone in my beauty college office, I heard loud and clear: "Marilyn, you're going to help women!" I sat there and looked all around and out the bay window, thinking I was going nuts. Again, I heard, "You are going to help women!" My answer to that voice, which I now believe was the Lord: "You picked the wrong one, buddy! I live here in Rancho Bernardo! I don't get muddy feet, and I AM helping women! I have a VERY BUSY life! I have not had over one thousand students!" I had just finished two years of college, and a professor named Barbara, with whom I had become a good friend, said she thought I was on a spiritual path. I freaked out and said, "I don't want to be a monk!" I didn't know it then, but the voice I heard in the office was the voice of God and the beginning of my spiritual path.

In the years that followed, I would attend seminary, graduate, and be introduced to Nancy Houtz, the Program Director of Prison Ministry at Wellspring Church. She and I discussed the prison ministry, and I met with women in the Vista Jail. That was my introduction to jails, prisons, and even death row at Chowchilla Prison in California. I became a prison chaplain commissioned by Wellspring Church outside of San Diego and spent the rest of my seminary years ministering to incarcerated women. At the time, I received an e-mail from a woman who wrote, "I am being released from prison, Marilyn. I want to attend your church and find you to counsel me." At that point, I knew I had my calling from God.

Through the sale of the beauty college, the House of Sophia was purchased, and so began this incredible journey of helping hurting women for twenty years.

Part II

The House of Sophia & Residential Home Preliminaries

Chapter 2

New Beginnings

After selling my beauty college, I purchased a beautiful home for hurting women. I wanted to surround them with the grace and beauty of God's nature. It had many amenities; a pool, Jacuzzi, and sauna. There were five bedrooms, five baths, a large exercise room, pecan and pomegranate trees, squirrels and birds, and a large tarp where we could hold Bible studies and parties for the homeless children. We found a food bank and had an abundance of fresh vegetables and fed a crowd of people. We named our home House of Sophia, meaning—House of Wisdom. My goal was to teach the residents how to become Proverbs 31 women.

I was able to purchase this home at a very reasonable price. Soon I realized that the amenities were beneficial to the ministry. There was enough space for indoor exercise, including a pool for working sore muscles. The Jacuzzi and sauna helped the process of detoxing. The yard and trees provided a tranquil place for praying, studying, or just reflecting. Residents were free to relax and cry about their old lives as they dealt with the remnants and pain of transformation to their new reality.

We also used our yard and pool to host Bible studies and dinners for our families, friends, and neighbors. This was a way for our clients to serve, make new friends, and a new way of life. Though such gatherings involved hard work, they were well worth the effort. We were close to a seminary, and many students helped with the work. People from area churches came on board as well. This is one way in which the ministry could make good use of volunteers. *Caution:* you must keep your focus and activities on *your* ministry. Others may want to use your home, yard, or pool for their pleasure. Some wanted me to use my talent for hair care in various ways unrelated to the ministry. Though I was a people-pleaser, I lost friends when I had to say no to these requests. I also lost energy for the ministry to my clients. When that happened, I became cranky, and we all felt the pressure.

Looking out into our community, we found a large food bank. I called them and made an appointment. After a very long-time gathering information, 501(c) (3), they determined our ministry was truly in need of their help. I soon made some wonderful, helpful friends who had other ministries and connected me with more resources. As the ministry grew, we could feed more people with our food alliance and eat very well. Today, you may be able to do much of this work online. The food bank was a great and helpful experience for me. The residents and I loved to shop there.

To be sure, God gave us some special advantages with the home, the seminary, and churches so close to us. You may not have the same situation; perhaps you don't want to work in this kind of environment. In any case, we can grow where we are planted. Search, ask, and find where your resources are, and help will come. Spend a lot of time praying (I learned this the hard way). You must take time to pray, or you will have no joy, peace, or strength to get your wonderful new ministry off the ground.

Chapter 3

Legal & Necessary Start-ups

Starting a business is complex and requires attention to detail. The legal issues include, but are not limited to, the following: Insurance, budgeting, accounting, selecting a board of directors, selecting a church sponsor, obtaining a 501(c) (3), choosing a bank that works with non-profit corporations, and obtaining a license for your residential program that is required from city hall. A DBA (Doing Business as Fictitious Business Name) Statement must be published in the local newspaper for several weeks under Legal Notices.

Your state may require different legalities. Go to the library or online and request information for a residential program in your state or region.

1. Insurance
Your church mentor, pastor, or elder could help you find who the church is using for their insurance and see if it will be possible to purchase your insurance from the church's insurance company. This could save you a lot of money. Also, you should know that

you are with a reputable company. We include a sample copy of our insurance and what was covered (Appendix to this chapter). This is outdated material. It is better to pay a little more for a reputable insurance company than to use a fly-by-night company that may be out of business next year. This is a word of caution.

2. Budgeting

When you work with a 501(c) (3), it is vitally important to have a Certified Public Accountant. He or she should have many references, hopefully from church members and people that you know. This is important because the church and your donors, and the IRS will be watching you very closely to see how you are spending the funds, which they have a right to see regularly. **DO NOT** use a bookkeeper no matter how good they are, because if and when you are audited, and you probably will be, remember you are using tax-free dollars, and it is your responsibility to use the funds wisely. The funds do not belong to you; they belong to the organization. The board of directors should give their approval to any purchase larger than $200.

I include outdated sample budgets and material (Appendix to this chapter) to help you set up your budget if needed.

3. Selecting a Board of Directors

Much prayer and foresight will be needed for this task.

1. The candidates for the board must be Christians. They must be mature in the faith, very godly, with a heart and understanding for your ministry vision and a long-term commitment to leadership. You yourself will be the founder/executive director. List your qualifications. Example: Mine were Biblical Counselor, MA., business owner, founder of a beauty college, and parenting. As I was the HOS founder/executive director, I did not go on the board of directors, but my attorney later informed me that I should have been on the board.

2. The next step is to select your governing board to include a president, a vice-president, a secretary, and a treasurer, by law. These members, and any others you choose to be on the board, will be the voting members. I decided to have only those four because my president wanted a minimal board and many advisors. He believed you could accomplish much more with a smaller board, and we did. Although you may choose as many ADVISORS as you wish to be on the board, they will not be voting members. It would be helpful if the advisors included a financial person who will help direct you to donors. The advisor's group might consist of a theologian, a businessperson, your pastor, or your attorney. It would also be useful also to include other financial businesspeople who want to support your ministry. Include a person who is familiar with grant writing and will be able to write grant proposals, attend seminars, and apply for grants as you expand your

ministry. This will keep your ministry healthy and fluid.

When you become more aware of your own weaknesses and your particular ministry's desires, you will need other advisors to come alongside you. Your voting board members are there to oversee and vote. You should have board meetings no less than every three months. You should reward your board members generously with dinners prepared or luscious desserts, as they will become fast friends and look forward to their evenings together accomplishing goals. Prepare an agenda beforehand, and check with your president and vice president to see if they need anything to be added to or deleted from the agenda. See a sample of an annual minute's meeting on page 16.

4. Selecting a Mentor

Select a mentor who will be your role model and teacher, who will have his or her ears and hands in every activity in the church and is warmly welcomed by all. The mentor should be able to teach you who to approach and how to approach them. He/she should even be willing to go with you or speak for you when you are looking for board members, insurance agents, or any other advisors to help you in your new ministry. The mentor should also be a good friend and be able to exhort you when that is needed. You should respect their advice, keeping in mind it is not meant as a criticism, but for your good. Such a mentor will be a good friend.

5. Obtaining a 501(c) (3)

Obtaining a 501(c) (3) is necessary, and it can be an expensive and challenging task. If you pay someone to make the arrangements, it can take up to a year or more. Approval is not guaranteed when submitted the first time, and often, additional fees are incurred. If you are going to pay someone to assist you, be sure to shop around and get a solid contract with these items addressed: How long will this take, and what is the final cost? By all means, you should get references. Several years ago, a paralegal told me that the going rate was $2,500 +. I had a friend, Nancy Houtz, who had her own ministry and who had written her own 501(c) (3). She was my original mentor and volunteered her services at no charge. One of my advisors, an attorney, looked it over, made a few small changes again for no charge, and received our document within three months.

Before we proceed to our next step, we need to name our new ministry. This will be necessary to submit your 501 (c) (3). (If you choose a name that starts with an "A" and choose a short name, you will always be at the top of every list that comes out). Your next step is to file for a provisional name and apply for your residential business license at city hall. This task needs to be published in a local newspaper for several weeks. Newspapers usually do this job very inexpensively.

6. Choosing a bank

Our final step is choosing a bank that works with non-profit corporations. **DO NOT use** your personal bank for your ministry bank. If you do, and any funds are moved from one account to the other account, called comingling, your 501(c) (3)'s license would immediately be removed. I speak from firsthand experience; it happened to me. The bank immediately called and informed me of what could happen. I called my board. A board member, also a church elder immediately went with me to his bank, which worked with 501(c) (3) and knew the rules and regulations. We then opened a checking and savings account for our ministry at my elder's bank.

**MINUTES OF ANNUAL MEETING OF
BOARD OF DIRECTORS AND MEMBERS OF
HOUSE OF SOPHIA
A CALIFORNIA NON-PROFIT RELIGIOUS CORPORATION**

The Board of Directors of said corporation held a meeting at the time, on the day and at the place set forth as follows:

DATE:	Sunday, June 25, 2006
TIME:	7:00 p.m.
PLACE:	17071-A Rancho Bernardo Road
	San Diego, CA 92198

There were present at the meeting the following:

Tom Stephenson, President
Alexander Stanton, VP/Secretary
Dick LaFleur, CFO
Carmen LaFleur

Also present:

Marilyn McDonald, Program Director
Deborah J. Dewart, Attorney
Kittie Stanton, guest

The meeting was opening in prayer at 7:15 p.m. Tom Stephenson presided at the meeting and reported that a quorum was present. Alexander Stanton acted as Secretary, with the assistance of Debbie Dewart, attorney for the corporation.

ELECTION OF OFFICERS AND DIRECTORS

The following directors were elected at the meeting on June 22, 2005 for a three-year term:

Tom Stephenson
Alexander Stanton
Dick LaFleur
Carmen LaFleur

Marilyn suggested that we consider Luke Carr as a corporate director (he is currently in Africa). He has expressed his willingness and desire to be on the board. On motion duly made, seconded, and unanimously carried, it was

16

RESOLVED, that Luke Carr be invited to the next board meeting, and at that time, we can vote on his election as a corporate director.

The directors of the corporation then duly elected the following named individuals to the positions indicated:

President/CEO   TOM STEPHENSON
Vice President   ALEXANDER STANTON
Secretary   ALEXANDER STANTON
Chief Financial Officer   DICK LaFLEUR

Each officer so elected, being present, accepted his office and agreed to perform the duties required.

MINISTRY REVIEW AND PLANS

Marilyn McDonald expressed her appreciation to the people who have helped her with this ministry in many ways since it began seven years ago, including Debbie, Tom, Xan, Dick and Carmen.

Rancho Bernardo: There are seven women residents who have participated in the House of Sophia program since January 2006: Sarah, Charlene, Elissa (now back in Florida near her family), Mildred (elderly woman in Escondido), Marla, Candace (recent graduate who brought her baby with her), and Arlene (current resident waiting for sentencing on DUI charge). There is a flier with brief descriptions about five of them. A prior resident, Kellie, who was once on the streets, is now married to a Christian man and has a new baby.

Africa: Dick LaFleur reported on the work in Africa. The corporation is providing regular financial support for the work of Reverend Dimba ($200/month, paid quarterly). He is headmaster of the Bible school in Malawi. There are 37 students learning the Bible and doing ministry/evangelism in the community. Eight Muslims have converted to Christianity. The ministry includes feeding about 2,500 people during a famine. An orphanage has been built, and there are currently 46 orphans. Marilyn asked if the board would consider an extra $50 per month to help feed and clothe these children. Reverend Dimba would oversee the use of these funds. On motion duly made, seconded, and unanimously carried, it was

RESOLVED, that the corporation will send an additional $50 per month to Reverend Dimba for the purpose of feeding and clothing the children in the African orphanage.

Florida: Marilyn had her condominium for sale for awhile, but it did not sell. She has decided to take it off the market, possibly rent it during the winter when rents are higher, and use it for ministry people the rest of the year as opportunities arise.

MINISTRY FINANCES

Marilyn reported that the corporation is free of credit card debt, and there is more money in the bank ($1,116 in checking plus $4,800 in money market) than there are bills to pay.

INSURANCE

The corporation's insurance policy has $1 million (per claim) coverage for officer/director liability, but no premises liability. Debbie suggested that we check into the price of adding premises liability insurance.

SDGE DISCOUNT PROGRAM

The corporation has qualified in the past for a 20% discount on the SDGE rates for tax-exempt facilities that conduct group housing programs. SDGE has recently provided an application to continue participation in the program, because facilities are required to reapply annually.

There being no further business to come before the meeting and on motion duly made, seconded and unanimously carried, the meeting was adjourned with prayer at 8:45 p.m.

ALEXANDER STANTON
Secretary

TOM STEPHENSON
President

1. Sample Insurance Document

SCHEDULE OF BENEFITS

Accidental Death	$5,000
Accidental Dismemberment	$5,000
Aggregate Indemnity	$300,000
Accident Medical, Excess	$25,000
Deductible	$50

Covered Class
Volunteers & Participants

Covered Activities
Non Contact Sports

COVERAGE FORM ☐ CLAIMS MADE ☒ OCCURRENCE

GENERAL AGGREGATE	$ 1,000,000
PRODUCTS & COMPLETED OPERATIONS AGGREGATE	$ 1,000,000
PERSONAL & ADVERTISING INJURY	$ 1,000,000
EACH OCCURRENCE	$ 1,000,000
FIRE DAMAGE (ANY ONE FIRE)	$ 500,000
MEDICAL EXPENSE (ANY ONE PERSON)	$ 20,000
EMPLOYEE BENEFITS	$
	$

House of Sophia

House of wisdom, est.1999
Proverbs 24:3,4

2. Sample Board of Directors

Mailing address: 5 Vista Palm Lane 104, Vero Beach, FL 32962   Phone: (772) 564-1449

Marilyn McDonald
Founder/Executive Director
Biblical Counselor MA

GOVERNING BOARD

David Walson, President .
Businessman
Church Elder Emeritus

Virginia Nichols, Vice President
Author & Entrepreneur

Mary Frame, Director of
Women's Ministry - Florida

Patricia Vawter, Secretary
and Treasurer

ADVISORS

David Nutting
Senior Pastor, North City
Presbyterian Church

Reverend John Frame
Professor and Author

Debbie Dewart
Attorney at Law,
Seminary Graduate

House of Sophia is
a 501c3 non-profit
charitable organization
defined by the IRS
General ID#330909115

www.houseofsophia.com

"By wisdom a house is built and through understanding it is established; through
knowledge its rooms are filled with rare and beautiful treasures." - Provers 24: 3-4

3. Sample Budget

Description	2010 Projected Amount
Advertising	2000
Automobile Expenses	2,500
Bank Charges	300
Dues & Membership	400
Educational Materials	300
Food Supplies for Women	1000
Insurance – for home	1200
Office Supplies	150
Postage & Printing	200
Professional Fees	800 (taxes)
Repairs – home	100
Supplies – Household/women	500
Telephone/internet	900
Utilities	725
Subtotal Operating Expenses	*$11, 075*
Credit Card	2400
Marilyn McDonald Salary	18,000
Rent – House	6000
Total – Operating Expenses	**$37, 475**

Projected income needed is: $3,125 per month

Current income: $950 per month

Current Shortfall: $2,175 per month

Projected income from ladies: $375 {$400 if Church wants rental fee for office use}

3. Sample Budget

The Lord has continued to bless the House of Sophia during the past year as a very successful transition has been made from our former program to a major meals ministry program.

Blessings that were poured out on us this year:

* In March, Marilyn's health was restored.
* A loan modification enabled HOS to continue to work here in San Diego.
* Marilyn secured a part-time job.
*The transition to a food ministry was successful and the HOS continues.
* Marilyn has been enabled to continue with part-time counseling.

Trials that have helped us grow in our faith this year:

* Real estate problems.
* Marilyn's health.
* The lengthy process required getting all parties together for approval of the food ministry.
* Budget cut in half.
* Not understanding that the Lord did not want us to close the HOS, but to begin a new ministry.

Blessings that through God's grace we were able to pour out on others this year:

* Thirteen needy families are served on a regular weekly basis.
* Fifty families are being served monthly.
* Food supplied by HOS has enabled NCPC to lower costs related to fellowship activity.

Thank you's from Marilyn

* To the HOS Board.
* To our donor's.
* To our volunteers
* To North City Presbyterian Church.

AND MOST IMPORTANTLY TO OUR LORD AND SAVIOR JESUS CHRIST.

Chapter 4

Locating a Church

I cannot stress sufficiently the importance of locating a good church. The church is an indispensable partner to the work of the residential ministry. In choosing a church, consider especially the following principles:

1. *Biblical Base:* The church should not be one that specializes in promoting good feelings, but one that promotes knowledge and application of the Word of God. Therefore, the teaching and preaching should not focus on verses of Scripture taken out of context. Rather, it should show how each chapter and verse of Scripture is related to all the rest, how each emerges out of the whole biblical story, setting forth God's true nature and his work in the redemption of sin. This preaching and teaching will necessarily be Christ-centered: it will focus on who Jesus is and what he has done for us, applying his saving work to all areas of

human life. The church should affirm the convictions of the universal church of all ages, as summarized in the Apostles' Creed, https://www.cce l.org/creeds/apostles.creed.html.

2. *Support of Residential Ministry:* The church should encourage and support the residential ministry. They should be willing to guide you and pray for you. For this purpose, some pastors, elders, or other ministry leaders should be able and willing to give time to meet with you regularly. They should be excited about helping you to start your journey.

3. *Gifts to Assist the Ministry:* In your church, not only pastors and elders, but other church members should be willing and able to use their gifts to help the residential ministry. Some may help with yard work. Others may lead and participate in classes dealing with the Bible, marriage counseling, cooking, or crafts. They may help residents in developing life skills, acquiring GED certificates, and driving to school. They may provide transportation to swimming classes, beauty college mornings, and other activities. If the church is soundly biblical,

you can expect members to volunteer in these areas as you make these needs known.

I have not found a better booklet on this subject than Jim Newheiser's *Help! I Need a Church*. In that book, Newheiser deals with the questions.

- Why do I need a local church?
- What qualities should I look for in a church?
- What are the wrong ways to choose a church?
- Where can I get more help?

He also discusses several hard questions about the church.

Chapter 5

Training Volunteers & Helpful Resources

Training Volunteers

Letter to Prospective Volunteers:

Thank you for your willingness to be of service at the House of Sophia. We would like you to know as much about us as possible so that you can be useful. — useful in a way that will glorify God.

At the House of Sophia, we give refuge to women who need a chance to redirect their lives. Women in situations that require change. They get the opportunity to leave the "world" behind for a while and focus only on God. Every lady who comes to the HOS is an individual and has different needs, but one need that is universal is that we must live with a commitment to the authority of God's Word. The HOS's mission is to share God's Word with those that have lost their way and want to come back.

Rights for Volunteers

1. To know as much about HOS as possible: the clients (without giving personal details), the programs, and the policies.

2. Treated as a co-worker, not free help, nor as a prima donna.

3. Given a suitable assignment with consideration for personal preference, temperament, life experience, education, and employment background.

4. To continue on-the-job training, such as new information about new developments; training for greater responsibility.

5. To guidance, direction by someone who is experienced, patient, and well informed.

6. You have the right to a variety of experiences through transferring from one activity to another through requests.

7. You have the right to be heard, to participate in the planning, to feel free to make suggestions, and to be shown respect for your opinion.

8. You have the right to be appreciated for your service. We, the HOS, will show appreciation in the form of awards luncheons and through small gift-giving.

Code of Ethics for Volunteers

1. Be sure you genuinely want to help others (not self-serving). Know what you are doing is of great value to others. I Peter 4:9-10 (Genuine love is serving others).

2. Accept the rules. Do not criticize what you do not understand. Rules are there for a good reason. Proverbs 13:13 (God rewards obedience).

3. Speak up about what you do not understand. Proverbs 1:7 {Desire wisdom and instruction).

4. Be willing to learn. Good training is essential to do a job well. Proverbs 2:1-6.

5. Keep on learning. Know all you can about your agency. Welcome supervision. You will enjoy your job and complete what is expected of you. Proverbs 2:1-6.

6. Be dependable. Do not make promises you cannot keep. You are your word. Proverbs 19:9; Proverbs 20:6-7.

7. Be a team player. Find your place on the team. Ephesians 4:32; Galatians 6:2.

8. Remember that you are not getting paid. This is service that you offer to the Lord. You are being considered as if you were a valuable employee. You are very valuable. I Peter 1:7 (You are precious in His sight).

Sample List of Available Jobs and Descriptions for Volunteers

Intake Worker:

Qualifications _____

Skills _____

Ability to maintain confidentiality _____

Dependability (to keep appointments) _____

Training to be arranged _____

Report to coordinator early to schedule the briefing __

Helpful Resources

Resource Library in the House of Sophia:

Here are the titles of some books that will be helpful to you. Of course, the most important book is The Holy Bible itself, which should be readily available to all. Make sure that you have Bibles in several translations and adapted to various ages and levels of education.

Adams, Jay

The Christian Counselor's Manual; From Forgiven to Forgiving: Learning to Forgive One Another God's Way; Shepherding God's Flock: A Handbook on Pastoral Ministry, Counseling, and Leadership; Problems: Solving Them God's Way; Marriage, Divorce, and Remarriage in the Bible: A Fresh Look at What Scripture Teaches; How to Help People Change: The Four-Step Biblical Process.

Fitzpatrick, Elise

Idols of the Heart: Learning to Long for God Alone; Love to Eat, Hate to Eat; Overcoming Fear, Worry, and Anxiety: Becoming a Woman of Faith and Confidence; Will Medicine Stop the Pain?: Finding God's Healing for Depression Anxiety, & Other Troubling Emotions; Women Counseling Women: Biblical Answers to Life's Difficult Problems; Women Helping Women: A Biblical Guide to Major Issues Women Face.

Mack, Wayne

Anger & Stress Management God's Way: Your Family God's Way; Down, But Not Out: How to Get Up When Life Knocks You Down; The Fear Factor- What Satan Doesn't Want You to Know; God's Solutions to Life's Problems; It's Not Fair: Finding Hope When Times are Tough; Reaching the Ear of God: Praying More and More Like Jesus.

Peace, Martha

Where is God in All of This? Finding God's Purpose in Our Suffering.

Powlison, David

Changing Hearts, Changing Lives; Domestic Abuse: How to Help; Pre-Engagement: Five Questions to Ask Yourselves; Seeing with New Eyes: Counseling and the Human Condition through the Lens of Scripture.

Priolo, Louis

Getting a Grip: The Heart of Anger Handbook for Teens; The Heart of Anger: Practical Help for the Prevention and Cure of Anger in Children; Manipulation: Knowing How to Respond.

Pryde, Debi

Why am I angry?

Tripp, Paul David

*Age of Opportunity: A Biblical Guide to Parenting Teens;
War on Words: Getting to the
Heart of Your Communication Struggles.*

Tripp, Ted

Shepherding a Child's Heart.

Welch, Edward

*Addiction: A Banquet in the Grave-Discussion Guide;
Blame It on the Brain: Distinguishing
Chemical/Imbalances, Brain Disorders, and Disobedience;
When People are Big, and God is Small: Overcoming Peer
Pressure, Codependency, and the Fear of Man; Self-Injury:
When Pain Feels Good; Depression: The Stubborn
Darkness; Motives: Why Do I Do, the Things I Do?*

**Procedure for checking out a book on the Time
Card following the Morning Meeting:**
1. Receive an assigned book from the counselor.
2. Write the title of the book on the daily Time
Card.
3. When you are finished, return for check-in to
the counselor at the Morning Meeting.

Press Release

This is a sample Press Release, ready for you to copy with your own personal information. This will ensure easy publicity by local communication services for you. Contacts may include TV, newspapers, and radio stations.

House of Sophia
House of Wisdom est. 1999

Press Release

March 11, 2010
House of Sophia Undergoes Its own Transformation: While Still Seeking to Transform Lives

This spring, the House of Sophia (HOS) is reopening its doors as a day program for women struggling to overcome addiction, depression, and other emotional and spiritual needs. Formerly a comprehensive 24-hour residential program for mandated and voluntary participants, HOS will continue to offer a supportive, nurturing environment with Christ-based counseling and services available five days a week.

"The decision to change our structure from a residential to a day program was made prayerfully and motivated by a desire to reflect Christ to a greater number of women in our community," says · Marilyn McDonald, Executive Director of House of Sophia. "The House of Sophia has always offered hurting women a place of peace and serenity. With our new format, we hope to develop emotionally strong, personally responsible and spiritually resilient women who can carry the peace and joy of Christ into their own homes."

Under the new structure, each three-month session will meet Tuesday through Friday from 10:00 a.m. to 4:00 p.m. and require church attendance on Sundays. Individualized programs are designed to treat the mind, body, and spirit through Bible study and prayers, counseling, exercise outdoors, goal setting, computer and education assistance, crafts, field trips, and volunteer-led courses on nutrition and cooking.

"The women that come to House of Sophia have seen so much ugliness in their lives. We want them to see and experience beauty," says McDonald, explaining why so much of the day is spent outdoors and on field trips to destinations like parks, the pool, and a beauty college. "Our primary goal is to help women recognize their need for God's grace and bow to Christ as Savior and Lord. In Him, they will find true beauty and become truly beautiful themselves."

Founded in 1999, House of Sophia is a Christ-based recovery program that has served more than 100 women from local churches, out of prisons, off the streets, and from drug-rehabilitation programs.

Deriving its name from the Greek word for wisdom, House of Sophia bases its philosophy of ministry on Proverbs 24:3-4- "By wisdom a house is built and through understanding it is established; through knowledge, its rooms are filled with rare and beautiful treasures." HOS only accepts women who are professing Christians and seeks to restore them to productive, godly lives.

Marilyn McDonald, founder and executive director of House of Sophia, has a degree in counseling from Westminster Seminary in Escondido, CA, and twelve years' experience as Chaplain of Women's Ministries. Viewing her own life as a miraculous story of recovery from years of abuse, depression, and drug dependence, Marilyn relates personally to HOS women and their struggles.

For more information about the House of Sophia, please E-mail: Marilyn.McDonald@sbcglobal.net.

PACT

Community Resource Directory
San Diego

"Gateway to Success"

Parole and Community Services Division is committed to helping parolees successfully re-integrate into the community.

Community Resources:
Contact Hospitals, Senior Centers
And Government Agency Resource centers.

Revised 3-1-2007

Rancho Bernardo Senior Services

16769 Bernardo Center Dr. Ste K-14
San Diego, California 92128
(619) 487-2640

HOME HELP LIST

Samples

Please Note: This is not an endorsement by the RB Senior Services, Inc., which has no affiliation with these individuals. RB Senior Services, Inc. assumes no responsibility with regard to services provided by these individuals.

California Samples

COMMUNITY RESOURCES

Abuse Reporting Lines:

Adult Protective Services	1-800-510-2020
Domestic Violence	1-888-305-7233
Child Abuse	1-800-344-6000
Ombudsmen (65 years+ in SNFs & RCFEs)	1-800-640-4661
Community Care Licensing	(858) 467-2367

If the Elder or Dependent Adult appears to have mental health problems call:

The Crisis Line (Crisis & Suicide Intervention)	1-800-479-3339
Seniors Teams (55 years+)	1-800-510-2020
The Access Line (Mental Health Services)	1-800-479-3339
APS, Inc. (55 years+ for Mental Health Case Mgmt)	(619) 283-5731

If a family member or caretaker says the elder or dependent adult has Alzheimer's/Dementia:

Alzheimer's Association	1-800-660-1993
Southern Caregivers Resource Center	1-800-827-1008

If a family member or caregiver appears to need assistance caring for an elder or dependent adult:

Aging & Independence Services	1-800-510-2020
Case Management	
In-Home Supportive Services	
Homemaker Referrals	

Special Populations/Needs:

Access Center (Disabled)	(San Diego)	1-800-300-4326
	(North County)	(760) 591-9156
San Diego Center for the Blind		(619) 583-1542
Deaf Community Services		(619) 682-5001
	(TDD)	(619) 682-5000
San Diego Regional Center (Developmentally Disabled)		(858) 576-2938
Senior Legal Services		(858) 565-1392
Battered Women's Services		(619) 239-0355

Many above services are available at no cost, or on a sliding scale

AGING & INDEPENDENCE SERVICES
COUNTY OF SAN DIEGO • HEALTH AND HUMAN SERVICES AGENCY

California Sample
Resource Guide

**A directory to assist single
parents and displaced
homemakers in
San Diego.**

Compiled by New Horizons Program
San Diego City College and Continuing Education

HOTEL/ MOTEL RATES FOR THE ESCONDIDO AREA

1. **Best Western Escondido**
   1700 Seven Oaks Road
   Escondido, CA
   (760) 740-1700
   $69.99 plus tax / Discount Rate for Hospital
   $89.00 plus tax/Regular Weekday Rate
   $99.00 plus tax/Regular Weekend Rate

2. **Comfort Inn of Escondido**
   1290 W. Valley Parkway
   Escondido, CA
   (760) 489-1010
   10% Discount Rate for Hospital
   $79.00 plus tax/Weekday Regular Rate
   $99.00 plus tax/Weekend Regular Rate

3. **Holiday Inn Express Hotel and Suites**
   1250 W. Valley Parkway
   Escondido, CA
   (760) 741-7117
   $89.00 plus tax Discount Rate for Hospital
   $99.00 plus tax Regular Winter Rate
   $114.00 plus tax Regular Summer Rate

4. **Motel 6**
   900 N. Quince Street
   Escondido, CA
   (760) 745-9252
   No discount rate for hospital.
   $49.99 plus tax for two persons/Weekday Rate
   $52.99 plus tax for two persons/Weekend Rate

5. **Sheridan Inn**
   1341 N. Escondido Blvd
   Escondido, CA
   (760) 743-8338
   $59.00 plus tax/Weekday/Discount Rate for Hospital
   $69.00 plus tax/Weekend/Discount Rate for Hospital
   $69.00 plus tax/ Regular Weekday Rate
   $79.00 plus tax/Regular Weekend Rate

6. **Super 7 Motel**
   515 W. Washington Avenue
   Escondido, CA
   (760) 743-1443
   No discount rate for hospital.
   $39.00 plus tax /Weekday Rate for one bed
   $49.00 plus tax / Weekend Rate for one bed

Please note that these rates may vary from season to season.
   nki/6-01

CANCER SUPPORT GROUPS-SAN DIEGO/NORTH COUNTY

BREAST CANCER

Breast Cancer Support Group meets Mondays 10-11:30 PM alternate weeks. Contact Judy Reynard, LCSW at (619) 437-4745 for location and more information.

Breast Cancer Support for Kaiser Permanente members 2nd & 4th Wednesdays 5-7 PM, 4647 Zion Ave, SD
For more details, (619) 641-4456.

Reach to Recovery- A volunteer visitation program. Information and support with a personal concern about breast cancer through the American Cancer Society, details call (800) 227-2345.

PPHS- "Rebound" Informational /support/exercise program. 7 weeks. Meets x2/week, PMC. Tuesdays and Thursdays 3:30 to 5:30 PM. Free of cost. Contact Kay Kimball, RN (619) 613-4044 or (760) 739-_3943. --

Health Concern- Support group only. Meets 1st and 3rd Tuesdays from 1PM to 2:30 PM. Meets 2nd and 4th Tuesdays 6:30 to 8:00 PM.

Stevens Cancer Center – Contact Ruth Wade for all details at (619) 626-6756.

Women's Cancer Task Force- meets last Monday of every month 7-9 PM, for more details call (619) 569-9283.

GENERAL, ADULT

Cancer Care Counseling Line – (800) 813-4673

PPHS – "Moving On" Informational /support/ mild exercise program. 7 weeks. Meets x2/week at PMC Tuesdays and Thursdays 3:30-5:30 PM; Free. Contact: Kay Kimball, RN at (619) 613-4044 or (760) 739-3943.

Wellness Community – Free program of Hope, Learning, and Friendship. 8555 Aero Dr #340, SD (619) 467-1065.

Cancer Connection – A community based program through the American Cancer Society, (619) 626-6762.

Cancer Care, Inc – Provides financial assistance to patients receiving Chemo, radiation therapy, and pain medication in the San Diego and Imperial Counties, also includes homecare, transportation, and childcare. For more details call (800) 813-4673.

People Helping People – Social meetings twice a month for cancer patients, families, and friends. Occasional speakers. Ramona and Escondido groups. Contact: Ellie Whitcomb (760) 789-0602. (This is a patient-run group. Facilitator has been a cancer patient but is not a health professional. She is a volunteer on the Med/Onc flr at PMC)

Support group for newly diagnosed patients contact Ann Wood, Ph.D. at (619) 554-2755 for more details.

Making Today Count - Support Group meets 1st and 3rd Thursdays 5:00-6:30 PM @ Kaiser, 4647 Zion Ave
SD, contact Priscilla Porter at (619) 641-4456.

WE PROUDLY WELCOME
Marilyn McDonald
House of Sophia

THE SUN SIGNATURE - MARCH 2010

"Women in Business"
March 2010

Ladies, need to restart your life?
Maybe the House of Sophia can help you.

By Nancy Canfield

FREE PRESS Opportunity

GUIDANCE- With religion and a sense of purpose behind her, Marilyn McDonald's aim in life is to help women get through abuse and depression and give them new objectives for success and independence. Left to right: Carmen LaFleur, board member, holding a book entitled *Inspired By A Child of God called Marilyn*; Marilyn McDonald and Virginia Nichols, class facilitator, holding a health and nutrition book to be used in their class.

House of caring

By Darcy Leigh Richardson
TODAY'S LOCAL NEWS

Marilyn McDonald started House of Sophia, a Christian recovery home for women, 10 years ago. Her goal is to restore women to being healthy, productive members of society. Peggy Peattie | Union-Tribune photos

Andrea B. (left), a recent graduate of House of Sophia, talks with board member Carmen LaFleur. Brown stayed at the Escondido facility while she recovered from viral encephalitis. Brown didn't graduate from high school, but with McDonald's encouragement, she is now studying to earn her GED.

FOOD DISTRIBUTION MINISTRY

Friday October 14, 2016

North City Presbyterian Church
11717 Poway Road
Poway, California

Set up: 12:30 pm

Food Distribution: 2 pm until gone

Volunteer help welcome

For Information: (858) 204-5255

"Lord, when did we see you hungry and feed you, or thirsty and give you drink?".... And the King will answer them, "Truly, I say to you, as you did it to one of the least of these my brothers, you did it to me."

Later in the residential program, a food distribution ministry was added to the House of Sophia. The ladies learned to serve the community in three churches, feeding the needy. After they graduated, they were rewarded with food, free of charge.

Part III

The Residential Program

Chapter 6

The Enrollment Period

The prospective resident begins with a phone interview and then makes an appointment with the director to come to the residential home for an assessment. If found suitable for residency, she will sign the Discipleship Ministry Agreement Contract and be given a handbook with the nuts and bolts of how the program is run. She will then be assigned her move-in date.

In the assessment appointment, the prospective client will be with two people (and only these) from the house-ministry: the Executive Director and one Board member. The meeting can be a laborious, tedious, and time-consuming process, up to four hours. Take your time. This process can be and usually is, overwhelming to the client. Make sure there are only two people with her in a very quiet setting, perhaps an office. There is a great deal of material to be discussed. We seek to avoid the situation where the client later says, "You didn't explain that to me," or "That was not told to me." As you go through the contract and the Visitor

Agreement, all three of you should initial each part as completed and make sure it is fully understood. Tell the applicant that this is for their protection and that of the home. Smile and let her know that there is balance in the program, with plenty of rest, good eating, and enjoyable fun times, and making new friends who will be doing all of this with her.

Some of the things the Director and Board member should look for: the applicant's type of personality, ability to look at the person she is speaking to, ability to speak clearly rather than mumbling. You should ascertain whether she is on meds.

Before the enrollment period, certain policies of the house itself should be established. Determine what meds are permitted to the residents. In what cases should the house admit applicants who have been diagnosed with various conditions, such as schizophrenia? You must decide, before the enrollment period, what type of clients you want to enroll. I had to learn the hard way. I lost a whole house of clients when we mixed drug addicts with schizophrenics. Those two groups do not mix well, in my opinion. This combination leads to a lack of harmony, and the dynamics of each group is very different from the other. You could take one group for a period of time and the other for a later period. At one point, I worked with the disabled after I had more schooling. I do not think that your ministry will grow rapidly if you try to take on too much too soon.

There are different needs for each group, and the finances are different.

Before the enrollment period, you must also decide whether you will use government funding and work on a sliding scale. The HOS rejected government funding because our intention was to be strictly biblical. My seminary degree is in biblical counseling. I am so pleased that after twenty years, I became that type of counselor. The bible gives us pure truth from the love of our Lord. There are wonderful biblical counseling centers like the Institute for Biblical Counseling and Discipleship in San Diego, and there are many good seminars offered within the biblical counseling movement for continued training.

I have emphasized the enrollment period because many who would start such a ministry would like to take every client the Lord sends to them. I wanted to do this; as I have said, I am a people-pleaser. But this is not advisable in a home residential program. Possibly, after you have had much training and have had experience in several homes, you might be able to open doors to every applicant. But you should not try to do this in a new ministry.

This information is food for thought in preparing for the enrollment of a client. The person you interview may be there by court order or because of an unhappy family situation. She may be grieving, sullen, or over-excited. Perhaps she looks at the program as a fun adventure, thinking it will be a piece of cake. Different applicants have a wide variety of motivations and attitudes. However, in every case, the client needs to be assured that the program is well organized and structured. She should understand that the requirements, if followed, will lead to graduation and a life that can be lived to the fullest with the Lord's help.

After you and the board member have decided that she is a fit for the program, a guided tour of the home is in order. Notify the current clients that a new prospective client will be looking through the home.

After the interview and tour, give the new client her entry date and a handbook containing the program's policies. She should also receive a list of what she is to bring in her suitcase, informing her that she should not bring anything else. Her suitcase will be thoroughly checked when she arrives, and then she must bring her handbook back with her or be charged for a new one. I am providing a complete table of contents and a few sample items to include in the handbook at the end of this chapter.

House of Sophia

The fear of the Lord is the beginning of knowledge;
Fools despise wisdom and instruction. *Proverbs 1:7*

HANDBOOK

House of Sophia Handbook

Table of Contents

WELCOME

Welcome to our home! We rejoice in the grace and providence of God in bringing you to our door and making room for you in our family. It is our earnest hope that you will eventually feel at home with us and consider yourself a part of our family.

Our purpose for accepting women, such as yourself, is to provide a loving family home. This is a place for women who are sincerely committed to overcoming their besetting sins (primarily with drugs and alcohol) according to the principles of the bible. This is a place for women to become intimately connected with the Lord and a local body of believers, where they may grow in the knowledge and grace of our Lord Jesus Christ becoming equipped to eventually leave the home and glorify God by leading productive lives in the community.

As you read the following pages, it may at first seem that we have a lot of rules and regulations. In fact, however, things are not nearly as legalistic as they may appear. It all depends upon your attitude, the new attitude the Lord has given you. You will find attitude is everything. If your outlook toward our structure is sour and self-pitying, you will soon become depressed and resentful over all the "do's and don'ts" asked of you. If, however, your attitude is positive and determined, and you view your new residence as an opportunity to grow, you will soon be filled with cheer and hopefulness. The Lord will bless you with a life that is rich with meaning, purpose, and productivity.

Two attitudes, in particular, will serve you well at The House of Sophia; an attitude of gratitude and an attitude of giving.

There is no greater recipe for failure, and no greater enemy to genuine Christian peace and joy, than a peevish and petty spirit. God has reached down in His wondrous grace to rescue us. Since we are the recipients of His grace and recognize that there was and is nothing in us to commend us to God, we - above all others, should be filled with gratitude, grateful that we have a new life to live to His glory.

While you are here, do not spend your time fussing, fretting, criticizing, and making others miserable with your petty complaints. "Do all things without murmuring and disputing" (Phi12:14). A critical and complaining spirit will only make you and your fellow sisters depressed and discouraged. Rather than complaining about the past or fretting about the future, spend your time thinking and speaking about all you presently have and all you are thankful for. "Give thanks in all circumstances" (Thess 5:8). Remember that a woman is and eventually becomes what she is constantly thinking about. "For as [a man] thinketh in his heart, so is he" (Prov 23:7; 4:23).

The second attitude that will help you live out your Christian faith here at House of Sophia is an attitude of giving! That is, giving of yourself by doing for others. Most of us have spent the greater part of our lives thinking only about ourselves, "My needs, desires, concerns," etc. And you can see where it has gotten us. Our lives have only become empty and miserable. Even though you may not at first understand it, you will soon find it is only when you start putting OTHER PERSONS before yourself, that is, thinking of their needs and their concerns, that you will begin to become the stable and happy woman God created you to be.

Jesus said it best: "It is more blessed to give than to receive" (Acts 20:35). To put it simply, we cannot get or grow until we first learn to give. That is a universal law that we can ignore only to our own detriment. These two attitudes - Gratitude and Giving - do not come naturally; they require daily effort and discipline on our part. But they are the only way of growing out of our miserable, self-inflicted addictions and into the wonderful life God has in store for each of us.

We, the Staff of the House, look forward to working with you and helping you to become the woman of God that you want to be.

We will do everything possible to give you the discipleship, encouragement, and support you need, but we will need your cooperation.

With the right Christ-like attitude, you will find that keeping "all the rules" is the least you can do in response to His grace shown to you in Christ.

On Behalf Of, The House of Sophia Staff & Marilyn McDonald, Director

Schedule of Activities

- 5:30 am: Wake-up/Personal Hygiene
- 6:00 - 7:00 am: Bible Study
- 7:00 - 7:30 am: Exercise (Marilyn McDonald, Director)
- 7:30-8:30 am House Meeting: plans, chores, duties, work schedules, activities for the day, needs request,
- Grievances – all discussed and finalized
- Prayer follows discussion (Marilyn McDonald, Director)
- 8:30 am – 9 am: Breakfast at residence
- 9 am – 5:00 pm: On-site Work (housekeeping chores / shopping etc for those without jobs)
- Off-site Work (regular jobs in business regular jobs in Christian families)
- Special Needs:
  - court dates
  - obtain social security cards &
  - drivers licenses
  - domestic violence classes
  - medical needs (dental/venereal/hepatitis C)
  - transportation arranged by Director
- 9:00 am - 8:00 pm Counseling: all day Thursday.
- 9:30 am - 11:30am New Life Presbyterian Church Bible Study
  - Wednesday for non-working residents
- 1 pm - 3 pm Crafts, sewing, cooking classes
  - Tuesday only for non-working residents
- 4 - 5 pm: Quiet time.
- 6 - 7 pm: Dinner at residence.

EVENING SCHEDULE (7:00 - 9:00 pm)
- Lights out at 10 PM
- Wednesday: Video/Classical music night.
- Thursday: Couseling with Ellen Scipione (a Volunteer and Certified Biblical Counselor) & Marilyn McDonald (Director)
- Friday: Bible Study and Counseling with Pastor Jose Rayas and his wife, Valerie (a licensed Social Worker)

Rules and Regulations

General Rules and Expectations:

1. Residents may bring one bag of personal belongs. There is not adequate storage space for more.
2. If resident leaves without notice, personal belongings will be stored by Staff for 30 days then given to the Salvation Army.
3. No use of illegal sustances, non-prescriptive drugs, or alcohol during your stay, with the exception of approved pain relievers. All medication will be given to staff and will be administered as prescribed.
4. Smoking is not allowed in the House or on the grounds at any time during your stay.
5. Verbal or physical abuse will not be tolerated at any time.
6. Use of the telephone is a privilege. Any long distance phone calls outside of San Diego County must be approved by the Director prior to making them. Phone calls should not exceed ten minutes.
7. Residents must attend the evening meal at 6:00 p.m. unless excused by Staff. If a resident cannot be home on time for a dinner, that resident should call ahead and a plate will be set aside.
8. Residents are responsible to check the Dinner Schedule to note the times they are scheduled for cooking and dishes. It is the resident's responsibility to find a substitute if she knows in advance that she cannot be there to fulfill her listed time(s)
9. Residents are responsible for their own wake up times and bedtimes.

> Morning Wake-up Times:
> Monday-Friday 5:30 AM
> Saturday 9:00 AM
> Sunday 7:30-8:00 AM, or in time for church.
>
> Evening Bedtimes:
> Sunday-Thursday 10:00 PM
> Friday-Saturday 12:00 Midnight

Personal Hygiene Expectations

1. Residents are expected to maintain good personal hygiene.
2. Residents are to keep their bedroom area clean and neat. Beds made, clothes picked up. etc.
3. Bedroom doors are to remain open at all times.
4. Each resident must clean up after herself. If you make a mess in the bathroom, bedroom, living room, kitchen, dining room, pool area or anywhre, clean it up! A messy, cluttered dirty house will not be tolerated. This is a good habit to develop as it will benefit you when you get into your own home.

SANITATION

1. All dirty dishes will be rinsed and put into the dishwasher to be washed so that any germs will be killed.
2. Bathroom sinks will be thoroughly cleaned after each use. Plain dishwashing soap is sufficient to kill germs.
3. Residents will not share toothbrushes, glasses or other personal items. If you don't have the items you need, ask Staff.

SPIRITUAL EXPECTATIONS

1. Bible studies in the House are mandatory for all residents unless excused by Staff. Respectful attention and participation are highly desireable. Bring your Bible, notebook and pen. Remain until the group is dismissed. The usual time for Bible studies is 6:00 AM each morning Monday - Friday and 7:30 PM Monday - Friday.
2. Residents are expected to maintain times of personal devotin and Bible study apart from the routine House Bible studies.
3. Required reading of inspirational books and other assigned homework related to your faith is expected to be completed within the timeframe allotted.
4. Residents are expected to spend at least two (2) hours a week in one-on-one discipleship with Staff. One of those hours will be scheduled and faithfully maitained.

What to Bring with you to House of Sophia

- Heavy sweater (for outings)
- Bathing suit
- 2 pairs pajamas, robe, slippers
- 3 sets sweats and/or 3 shirts and shorts
- 2 Outfits for church
- 3 pair shoes, 1 tennis, 1 dress and one casual
- 1 comb or brush, toothbrush
- No more than 15 cosmetic items
- 1 picture
- 1 purse to be turned into Marilyn for inspection – along with all meds
- 1 bible, preferably NIV
- 1 journal and pencil (3 ring spiral)
- $50 spending money
- $107.75 for sea silver vitamins

Some other Rules

- No smoking
- No talking to neighbors or coming to Marilyn's house without invitation

This Is Not A 24 Hour Watched Facility. Your Crisis Is Not My Crisis. You will have three hours in the morning to talk with me and spend most evenings with me. Your time to make requests is at the morning meeting. It is a privilege to be at The House of Sophia for you and for us.

Chapter 7

The First Thirty Days/Nutrition

*Put off your old self, which belongs to your former manner
of life, corrupt through your deceitful desires. Be renewed
in the spirit of your minds, and put on the new self, created
in the likeness of God in true righteousness and holiness.
Ephesians 4:22-23 (ESV}*

The first thirty days are crucial to the complete
program. It is the removal of all outside stimulation.
The contract has been completed. The client is very
nervous, excited, scared, and possibly very ill,
needing some detoxing. It is extremely important to
spend the first thirty days with the client to care,
counsel, study her needs, and start healing the body
with good nutrition. This is also the time for healing
of the soul. It is the introduction to Jesus, the
beginning of "putting off" the old ways of life and
"putting on" the new ways of the godly woman.

Our client would arrive the night before, unpack
her suitcase, and then get up at 5:30 the next morning.
Exercise at the House of Sophia proved to be effective
at calming the nerves, relieving depression, and
creating a healthy body. It is a silent time to prepare

the heart, reflect, and enjoy nature and God's gifts. Depending on the weather, we took a mile walk, watched exercise videos, or swam. After our exercise, we introduced the clients to the daily schedule.

At 7 a.m. was our Morning Meeting. At our morning meeting, we discussed plans for each client's day and shared grievances. Female necessities were put on a list to purchase, and appointments and personal counseling were set up. We discussed food allergies. Any other conversations they wanted to have were permitted. This was an open group meeting.

At 7:30 a.m., we had a very small Bible study that started with introducing the book, How to Grow in Christ [1], and then we proceeded to breakfast, meds, and vitamins. At 9:00 a.m., we discussed daily tasks and daily activities.

For the first 30 days, we did everything together. If one went to the doctor, we all went. I stayed with them continually. We discussed our daily tasks and activities altogether and then started them at 10:00 a.m. On their first day, each was given a journal to write her short-term and long-term goals, her life story, and anything else she wanted to write about (desires, dreams, how she was feeling, problems with health, etc.) In each counseling session with me, they would share what they had written in their journal if they could. Some could not even write in the beginning. Some just needed to be in bed. These

---

[1] By Jack D. Kinneer (Phillipsburg, NJ: P & R Publishing Co., 1981).

journals were very helpful because many wrote their life stories and showed me their level of education, motivation, desires, willingness to work, and many other things that I learned from the timecards and journals. From there, I could discern if they were in a dark place, if they were getting ready to run, or if they had suicidal thoughts.

We used videos to help women who were having difficulty focusing for long periods of time (a common side effect of drug use and learning disabilities that need visual stimulation). Learning about their various learning styles helped them with personal growth. The video lesson also taught them teamwork and encouraged discussion. They watched a video of Matthew one day, Mark the next, and subsequently, Luke and John. As they watched these, they could discuss them as a group and take notes together, but at the end of the week, after watching the videos several times, they were each expected to present their own separate paper comparing and contrasting the four gospels. One client's compare-and-contrast paper read, "The four gospels all had different names and they were all in the Bible," but in time, their understanding of the Bible grew deeper.

The Passion of Christ DVD was used to show them the gratitude that we should have for Christ's sacrifice and not view our own sin too lightly because we are covered by grace. While this movie is graphic in nature and has unbiblical parts, those issues were discussed and pointed out to teach a lesson on discernment.

The Bible Promise Book[2] was given to each client. It had a table of contents that dealt with many common heart issues, i.e., anger, children, trust, etc. When a client was dealing with a particular heart issue, we would turn to that page in the book and read all the Scripture that God had given us regarding that issue. Through this, we would learn that God speaks to us through His Word, and has given us His promises, and wants us to pray for one another.

As they began to eat healthy meals, exercise, learn about Jesus Christ, and practiced the right things, "putting off" the old way of life and "putting on" a new way of godly living, God poured out blessings and gave grace and mercy to His children. The Proverbs 31woman uses her hands wisely: makes things for her family, shops wisely, travels for bargains, networks with other women, takes care of herself, relaxes, and meditates on God. Likewise, the women in their first thirty days network by bonding with other Christian women and develop their industrious character in craft classes by working with their hands to create things for their homes and gifts for others, such as braiding rugs, making jewelry, purses, birdhouses, Christmas ornaments, and Thanksgiving table decorations. Over the last eleven years, I had noticed these women when they came back from their craft classes, refreshed and psychologically ready to work on their next assignment. Shopping outings taught the women to

_____

[2] Uhrichsville,OH:Barbour Publishing, Inc.,1990.

shop wisely, stay within their budget, make healthy choices, plan ahead, and keep family meals in mind. This balanced our program so that it was about studying and learning to enjoy the things God has provided, learning to balance their life and become a complete woman.

When it was appropriate, very early in the first thirty days, we would all go to the beauty college and receive services, such as, pedicures, manicures, haircuts, and new hairstyles. We would often spend our summer evenings swimming and enjoying the Jacuzzi and sauna. New tasks were being added, such as making a proper bed, cleaning the bathrooms, laundry on Saturday mornings, and learning teamwork. We were completing our schedule for becoming a godly woman.

We were now beginning to look at the women seeing themselves a little differently. They were starting to enjoy eating good healthy meals and loving their exercise. They were not missing their alcohol, drugs, and cigarettes as much. They were like tiny flowers growing out of the cement. There was the very beginning of hope. We were beginning to fulfill some court-ordered programs, to get doctors' appointments, to look at our short and long-term goals with hope, and time to start introducing them to good nutrition for energy, wellness, and a balanced lifestyle without drugs, cigarettes, and alcohol.

We began teaching good eating (NO SUGAR, NO WHITE FLOUR, lots of fruits and vegetables, fiber and quality meat the size of the palm of your hand).

After studying your clients for 30 days, find out what they would like to have for breakfast and lunch. For their ideal day, what would they choose to have for breakfast, lunch, and dinner? For their homework, assign them to keep a food diary and then share their food diaries in class. Choose several examples from the clients and show them what would be a better choice. Their homework will be another food diary with comments on why they made their choices (convenience, taste, ingredients on hand, budget, or lack of cooking knowledge, etc.) Also, have them bring to their next lesson, a package or a container with the ingredients from one of the foods listed in their diary. We read and explained the labels they brought to class. The next assignment was to continue with the food diary and create a menu for each day for a week, using the menu format and weekly grocery specials. Through these activities, women learned how to shop economically. The women created their shopping lists from their menus and illustrated how to make a meal with leftovers. A recipe was written for them to cook. The next week they were to take that meal either to a shut-in or put it in The House of Sophia ministry freezer for future use of serving others. There were ongoing classes on cooking and nutrition throughout the program, not just the first thirty days.

Together with the other ministries, The House of Sophia was providing food to the homeless community. Three churches brought food to the homeless monthly. They received the food through the ministry of The House of Sophia. I was a member of a large food bank where we could obtain quality foods that had almost or recently expired. As a member, I could get all the food I wanted to be delivered to the places I needed for pennies on the dollar. During this time, the ladies from The House of Sophia had access to good quality food for free, even beyond their graduation. They could serve at the food distributions of the churches and take all the food they needed for no charge. This left them with no excuses for not eating well.

The owner of a nutrition store taught nutrition classes and was knowledgeable about the use of vitamins and herbs. We also had two nurses available who practiced holistic wellness with nutrition and vitamins. We were now trying to get the proper nutrition into our ladies. We worked with doctors and health food stores. We received donated boxes of vitamins.

Now our clients could apply for work, school, and attend their court-ordered, mandated programs. They were actually meeting their short and long-term goals. They were having some of their desires met and were also seeing their own bodies change. Due to our staff, volunteers, and board of directors who provided their time, knowledge, and finances, we were able to help them with physical check-ups and blood work. We located free clinics for our clients who had been incarcerated and needed detoxing. We also had a quality library in our home with nutritional resources to keep us updated with nutrition.

The House of Sophia Time Card

	Name	Date	Day
	_____	_____	_____

6:00 AM   Bible

7:00 AM   **Morning Meeting**

7:30 AM   **Exercise, Breakfast, Meds & Vitamins**

9:00 AM   **Tasks & Daily Activities**

10:00 AM

11:00 AM

12:00 PM   Lunch

1:00 PM

2:00 PM

3:00 PM

4:00 PM

5:00 PM

6:00 PM   Dinner

                 Evening Activity

Chapter 8

Program Overview

The resident will be shown love as God gives love, despite their pasts, and the knowledge that there have been crimes committed in most instances. The program offers: Spiritual guidance, financial responsibility, social responsibilities, parenting classes, guidance in marriage reconciliation, child visitation, and recreational activities as occasions arise. The residents will learn to earn their privileges and understand that this is not an entitlement program.

Residents must learn that there are rules that must be followed in every area of their lives, both personal and social, so that they will not repeat the same mistakes that created their problems to begin with. This is accomplished by having a highly structured requirement schedule that will be strictly adhered to.

The Program Offers:

Spiritual Guidance:

- Biblical discipleship, with several Bible studies and inspirational reading, is required each week.
- Personal encouragement
- Personal counseling

There is no dating during this time. There is no TV. There are monitored videos.

Personal Financial Responsibility:
- Learning to keep and balance a checkbook
- Budget planning and maintenance

Social Responsibilities:
- Good personal hygiene and the importance of it
- Regular exercises and good nutrition so they can adequately care for their bodies
- Personal boundaries for themselves and respect for others' property
- Job-hunting skills and resume preparation at the appropriate time
- Required church attendance serval times each week.

Home and Family:
- Homemaking skills
- Parenting classes and guidance in marriage reconciliation when applicable.

Chapter 9

Development of Responsibilities

Once the client has passed the first thirty days probationary period, she is expected to follow the rules and regulations outlined in the residency handbook and to record her individualized schedule on timecards. She is now "putting off" the old life and "putting on" her new life of responsibilities (Eph. 4:22-24) through a highly structured program in concert with godly mentors and volunteers who model exemplary character.

The result is that she has learned to use her time wisely. She has learned to appreciate the gifts of shopping, the opportunity to choose a good book or movie, talking to her children or husband on the phone, having a new Christian friend over for lunch, picking a fresh bouquet from the rose garden, and the blessings of just having breath and being alive. She is beginning to see the light and starting to see her future goals, knowing that she is a princess of the King. The client should now be showing some hope for the future. Hope is the main quality all of my clients had lost when they entered the HOS.

Many now desire to know more about our Lord and are gaining hope and knowledge of Him. When that hope and knowledge is acquired, the client becomes a teachable student. The staff will now see a glimmering spark of an attitude of gratitude and an interest in giving. To the staff, what a joy this is! They thank God for this budding flower of faith.

When you see hope and a thirst for knowledge, the client is now teachable and can assume more responsibilities. Caution: Go slow. Each student will grow at a different pace. Responsibilities and new tasks will come to each in a different order. The director will receive great help and knowledge from the timesheets. I've included three examples of completed timecards here.

Putting Off the Old and Putting On the New

As the student learns to trust you, she will acknowledge her sins to you, and you can help her put off old sins and put on her new godly life. We are not here to judge her or to be self-righteous. In this phase, we are to love and encourage. I would share some (not all) of my sins with her and show her how putting off and putting on helps me. I don't ask the client to document my sins. I mention them to let her know that I am a sinner. I do not want her to think that I am claiming to be righteous as if I was good, and she was bad. Rather, I seek a mutual understanding that builds trust. In this way, I let her know that this task is an ongoing process for all of us, and the process takes time.

This mutual understanding is based on Scripture. It is essential that your client understand your teachings come from the Bible. One helpful book in this regard is the Quick Scripture Reference Book by John G. Kruis. Several copies of this should be available in the house library to be checked out. This book makes it easier to find relevant Scripture references since the client may not, at this point, be able to find them in the Bible itself; she is just starting her journey in Scripture.

Your client is now looking at her own life as the beginning of a new reality. She will need much love. It will be beneficial to express that love in the daily morning prayer meeting, thanking the Lord for his mercy and grace, as you and she are seeing the changes in her life. The client is now starting to bud and is acting as a daughter of the King. Your joy will be in seeing the budding flower bloom and become a princess of the King.

Sample Time Sheet 1

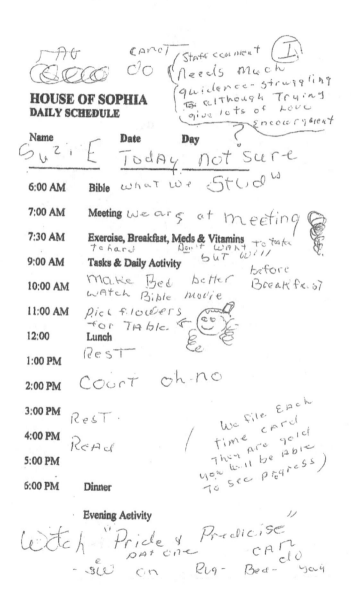

CANOT Staff comment
CO Needs much
guidence- struggling
To although Trying
give lots of Love
Encouragement

HOUSE OF SOPHIA
DAILY SCHEDULE

Name	Date	Day

Suzi E TodAy not sure

6:00 AM Bible what we Study

7:00 AM Meeting we are at meeting

7:30 AM Exercise, Breakfast, Meds & Vitamins
To hard   Don't WANt to take
                                    but Will

9:00 AM Tasks & Daily Activity
                                    before
10:00 AM Make Bed better BreakfAst
WAtch Bible movie

11:00 AM Pick flowers
for TAble.

12:00 Lunch

1:00 PM Rest

2:00 PM Court oh-no

3:00 PM Rest.
                    We file Each
4:00 PM Read   time card
                    They are gold
5:00 PM   you will be Able
                    To see progress)

6:00 PM Dinner

Evening Activity
Wtch "Pride & Predicise
pAt one   CATI
- siu on Rug- Bed- you

73

Sample Time Sheet 2

② more
advanced

HOUSE OF SOPHIA
DAILY SCHEDULE

Name   **Date**   **Day**

Cindy   2.10 ¹⁵   TUESdAy

6:00 AM   Bible How To grow in Christ

7:00 AM   Meeting Need-deorgant. hAs
                                              complaint

7:30 AM   Exercise, Breakfast, Meds & Vitamins
                  A little cold outside
9:00 AM   Tasks & Daily Activity

10:00 AM   Shower Ask for haircut
                  clean Room
11:00 AM contine reading
                  Trusting God
12:00   Lunch

1:00 PM   going Swiming

2:00 PM   counceling

3:00 PM

4:00 PM   help prepare dinner

5:00 PM

6:00 PM   Dinner

              Evening Activity

CrAfs clAss   cAll children
Read-   prAy- Vist with clients

Sample Time Sheet 3

(Advanced) 3
Student

HOUSE OF SOPHIA
DAILY SCHEDULE

(Stas
Remember go slow
probleme will
occur: often
Depresion
followe
didn't go as
expected)

Name	Date	Day
Mary Smith	March 5 - 2015	Thursday

6:00 AM Bible — Make serve coffee Tea for all
finish How to grow in Christ - finished

7:00 AM Meeting
paper what I learned
Ask about resenue - and work this book

7:30 AM Exercise, Breakfast, Meds & Vitamins
Love —

9:00 AM Tasks & Daily Activity
Want more To do - getting board

10:00 AM finished Weekle book ready to Test
doing own Laundry

11:00 AM Want Allourc - To start budget
Want more chores

12:00 Lunch

1:00 PM prepare for Dr. Appt

2:00 PM Dr Appt

3:00 PM wrap up 2nd month

4:00 PM ↓

5:00 PM Prepare for 1st outside visit with
Children (or Husband) only
Dinner

6:00 PM Dinner

Evening Activity

Exciting
Exciting   Movies   SP
call family   2 part pride & predice /

75

Put Off / Put On

*To **put off** your old self, which belongs to your former manner of life and is corrupt through deceitful desires, and to be renewed in the spirit of your minds, and to **put on** the new self, created after the likeness of God in true righteousness and holiness.*
Ephesians 4:22-24

PUT OFF

Abuse of Alcohol and Wine

SAmple

PUT ON

1 Cor. 6:15 Do you not know That your bodies Are members of Christ Himself.

Prov. 20:1 Wine is A mocker And beer a brawler: whoever is by Them is not Wise.

Chapter 10

Completing the Program

Once a resident has completed all her projects, tasks, class assignments, court appearances, goals set at the beginning of the program, and is an established member of a community church, there is a graduation party. Gifts, such as a car, items to furnish her home, continuation of food assistance until no longer needed, gift cards, and even a honeymoon or dream vacation are prepared for the BIG DAY.

Graduation Parties:

With our church elders, volunteers, family, and friends, more money gifts, designated for phone, rent, gas, and gift cards for movie tickets, bowling, beauty college haircuts/nails, Starbucks, and one local fun place such as a restaurant may be added. The opportunity to speak and congratulate is planned for all to participate, starting with the leaders, then volunteers, family, and friends. Finally, the director speaks to the graduate with a diploma and a formal announcement to begin opening the gifts.

After Bible study classes, the party is concluded with lots of hugs, well wishes, possibly a
Bible and/or other book and "Let's Eat!"

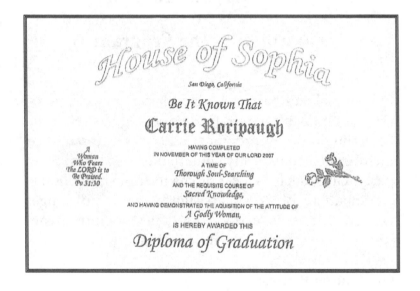

We were ready to issue Carrie her diploma and graduate her when she became so ill that she had to return home. There she went to be with the Lord. Carrie had become a robust Christian while in the HOS. So we issued her diploma to her in her eternal home in heaven.

Opening gifts for clients newly acquired apartment at her graduation gift party.

A graduate's continuing food assistance from the food bank for as long as is needed.

Part IV

The Golden Nuggets

Chapter 11

Do's and Don'ts

These are gold nuggets that will help you run a smooth and joyful program. You want persons of character with specific guidelines for the director/client relationship, volunteers to be well trained and appreciated. The overall goal is to help the residents discover their own strengths. We are not here to rescue them and leave them still vulnerable, but rather to walk alongside and encourage them.

Please remember this is how I handled real situations (or would have handled them today). These are suggestions only. There are many other do's and don'ts that I have not put in this book, and many have been covered in chapters other than this one.

We have had two small claims lawsuits. We won them because of our great contracts, which were CYA ("Cover your ass," as we say in the business world). For example, see my account of a complaint brought against us in Appendix B, following this chapter.

I use the Scripture text Proverbs 31 as our model for HOS.

Do's

1. Use time effectively. Let the client know when it is her turn to speak, and make sure each client has a turn. (I used a one-minute egg timer).
2. Remember that the client's crisis is not your crisis, unless she urgently needs to go to the hospital or has a death in her family.
3. Take a client aside or out for coffee and read some testimonials to her from previous clients. Call a past graduate to come and spend a day with her. If all else fails, go shopping.
4. Get permission and ask the client to share at the morning meeting. This is a way to build friendships.
5. We are a team and family, becoming godly Christians, so we help one another. As God is not a respecter of persons (Acts 10:34), we are equal in his eyes. So we should not divide the group of residents into opposing groups. The only two types of people are believers and unbelievers (Romans 8:5-8).
6. Encourage each client to become a decision-maker with the ability to make healthy choices with the Lord's help.
7. When a client tries to do something and it doesn't work out, help her figure out what went wrong and try again.
8. Admit to her that you will fail her, but God never will. To underscore this point, give her the small softcover *Bible Promise Book* by Eugene H. Peterson.

9. If a client leaves the program without graduating, wait for a span of time and then call or e-mail her pastor, mother, or husband to find out why she left. In one case, the answer was that the woman was "too lonely." The husband is now a deacon in the church, and this client is active as well. We communicate and love one another. I have included in Appendix A, following this chapter, some e-mail correspondence concerning another case that did not turn out so well.

10. In one sense, you should be willing to become a spiritual mother to your clients. Many of them will come to have a love/hate relationship with the program and want you to be their mom. Some have called me their spiritual mother, and that is fine. Indeed, it gives me great joy.

Don'ts

1. Don't allow a client to use the morning meeting for personal wallowing. Tell her to write out her complaint and save it for a counseling session.

2. Do not assume a client's heart-motives or interrupt her when she is speaking. Repeat what she said that you believed was wrong, dealing with any misunderstanding that may have arisen.

3. When a client complains of a crisis in a class session, do not stop the class immediately. Help her schedule a discussion of the problem on her timesheet.

4. Do not allow a client to give up.
5. Do not share anything with one client about another. All information is confidential, and if you betray confidentiality, it will hurt everyone's trust in you.
6. Do not allow a tattletale (1 Timothy 5:19-20) unless the matter is so severe that it needs to be dealt with immediately. Try to follow Scripture and maintain confidentiality.
7. Do not ever compare one student with another.
8. Do not try to make the client's decisions for them.
9. If the client makes a poor choice, do not rescue her, and do not shame her. These women are very immature, at best baby Christians, when they begin the program. But they are not your children, and you are not there to rescue them. You should not lead the clients to yourself but to Jesus Christ.
10. Do not become the client's God, or she will not make it in life. Eventually, she will realize this to be false, and you will not be her friend.
11. When a client is determined to leave and does, do not beg or try to stop her. Show her your love very clearly and encourage her to continue.

Conclusion

I have noted these dos and don'ts to caution you that the good, the bad, and the ugly will come. Would I do it all over again? Oh, yes, yes, yes! After all the challenges, I would do it all again.

I did not want to write this book, but many urged me to do it. Among them were seminary professors, counselors, my Board members, my mentors, and my friend Mary Frame. With sweat, anger, and tears, this book is for you, my friends, and now with much joy in my heart. There is not a book like this one on the market. It will benefit your new ministry because it comes out of my experience and the principles of Scripture. I wished I could have had this sort of book when I started HOS.

Please do not fear what is to come in your ministry. Here is the Scripture God gave to me at the beginning of this journey:

"For I know the plans I have for you — plans for good and not for evil, to give you a future and a hope." (Jer.29:11)

For other passages addressing our fear, see Appendix C, following this chapter.

My Lord has kept His promise, and I have grown, and the love of all the women is in my heart. As I approach age 78, He is still engaging me to work for Him. I give all the glory for this book to You,

My Heavenly Father,

My Abba Daddy,

My Wonderful Counselor,

I am your daughter.

Appendix A: Marilyn's E-mail Correspondence with a client who departed from the ministry

Marilyn:

"Now to him who is able to keep you from stumbling, and to present you faultless before the presence of his glory with exceeding joy,
To God, our Savior, who alone is wise, be glory and majesty, dominion and power, both now and forever. Amen." (Jude 1:24-25)

Client:

Dear Marilyn,

There is nothing in my heart against you. The Lord has mercifully, compassionately, and undeservedly rescued and delivered me, and I am grateful. I am continually awed and amazed at God's mercy and kindness. He truly sets the captives free! I will pray, and if the Lord brings anything to my mind that I believe He wants me to share with you, I will do it.

"He also brought me up out of a horrible pit, out of the miry clay, and set my feet upon a rock, and established my steps." (Psalms 40:2).

Grateful for God's abundant grace.

Appendix B: A Complaint Brought Against the House of Sophia

I will discuss a complaint letter as an example of how our residential home ministry dealt with a legal issue. That issue was very complicated, so I will not print the entire letter but will summarize the complaint and the steps we took in responding to it.

The client complained to the church that the program did not meet proper qualifications and did not deal appropriately with her very grievous sins. We responded as follows:

1. The church gave the complaint to my board. The board took action immediately.
2. I was asked to provide all information available, including reference letters from donors, the judge's court, and her social worker.
3. We included a list of items given to her, including many food gifts to children, nearly new bicycles for children's trips to another state, and marriage-counseling classes. They thought it would be impossible to restore their marriage, but God made that happen. In addition, she got a job, and our church gave her a car. She and her husband had become church members, and her husband was now in love with the Lord.

The results of the inquiry:

On our part: the court accepted the HOS program.

On her part: she took her husband and children and all we gave her, and I believe they went across the United States to escape obeying court orders. The husband could have stayed, for he had a good, well-paying job; but went away with his wife instead, to please her. That greatly saddened me.

In this situation, HOS, at an early point in its ministry, gave too much too soon and did not communicate with the church as we should have.

Appendix C: Scripture Passages on Overcoming Fear

1. Don't fear to follow the Lord because of your weaknesses and inadequacies. God's strength is made perfect in weakness. Be bold and move out for the Kingdom. 2 Corinthians 12:9; compare 3:5, 4:7, 16; 1 Corinthians 2:3-4; Rom. 8:26; Eph. 3:20; Acts 4:29; Luke 12:12; 2 Timothy 1:7; 2 Corinthians 2:14.

2. Don't fear that your past mistakes, sins, and failures will determine your future. Your sins are forgiven, and He works all things together for good. Leave your past regrets behind and head for the glorious future. Romans 3:23-26;

8:1, 8:28; 2 Corinthians 7:10; 1Timothy 1:15-17; Philippians 3:13-14.

3. Don't fear Satan's accusations, the world's hostility, the power of sin, or even death. The Lord has defeated them all. Make Jesus your Lord. Answer to Him. Zechariah 3:1-5; Colossians 2:15; John 16:11; 33; Romans 6:6; 11, 1 Corinthians 15:54-55; 1 Peter 3:14-15.

4. Don't worry about the future. God is sovereign, and He knows your needs, and He is your Father. Live today. Matthew 6:32, 34, 10:29; Hebrews 13:5-6; Luke 11:3; Philippians 4:19; 1 Peter 5:7.

5. Don't live with a sense of dread and fear. God's love surrounds you and defines your life. Lift up your head. Isaiah 54:9-17, 60:1; Psalm 3:3; Romans 5:5-8; 8:31-39; Ephesians 3:17-19; John 3:1; Galatians 4:4-7; John 16:27.

6. Don't be afraid that He hasn't heard your prayers. He always listens and answers prayer without fail. Ask and be carefree. John 14:13, 16:24; Luke 11:9-13; Philippians 4:6-7; 1 John 5:14-15; James 1:5.

7. Don't worry about changing what you cannot change. You can't save yourself or anyone else. But Jesus is a great Savior. He has added an eternity of days to your life. He can save anyone or any situation. Pray and expect. Luke 12:25-26; 18:26-27; Romans 4:19-21; John 11:25-26; Isaiah 63:1.

8. Don't worry about finding the Lord. He has already found you. You have all of Him, and everything that belongs to Him is yours. Rejoice and praise. Luke 15:4-6, Romans 10:6-8; 1 Corinthians 1:30; Ephesians 1:3; 2 Peter 1:3.

9. Don't be burdened with the things you have to do as if you had to do them in your own strength. The Lord is a very present help. Abide in Him. John 14:16-18, 15:5; Psalm 46:1; Matthew 11:28; Isaiah 46:3-4; 1 Peter 4:11; Philippians 4:13; Luke 12:12-30.

10. Don't worry about the things of this world. They are passing away. The Father has been pleased to give you the Kingdom. Give yourself away. Matthew 6:19; Luke 12:32-33; 2 Corinthians 5:15; Romans 12:1-2; Philippians 3:7-8; 1 Peter 1:4; John 15:12; 1 Corinthians 3:21-23; Colossians 1:12-14.

Chapter 12

Testimonials

The success of the House of Sophia for about twenty years is the work of our Lord and Savior Jesus Christ, a Bible-based church, and a Christian board of directors. This leadership upheld the Biblical philosophy of "putting off the old self and putting on the new self." (Ephesians 4:22)

Thank you for your awesome job. It was of the Lord and what I was praying for.

Dona

After leaving the HOS, this sweet sister went to be with the Lord. She became a godly woman while with us. I had the blessing of giving her eulogy.

Dear Marilynn— I'm so full of praise I don't know how to express it fully.

God is so good. And I thank Him greatly for the work He has done in you!

To God be the Glory.

It was so good to see September off most of the medication.

May the Spirit of the Lord dwell in us all continually

I yours in Christ,

Melonie Ames

Our client came in deaf, with a goal—to learn sign language and become a singer and dancer. Through a doctor's treatment, she recovered 80% of hearing in one ear. She then learned sign language, and became a sign language worship leader singer/dancer in a megachurch in full costume.

Tina had been in HOS for about three weeks.
She wasn't happy.

She went to school to learn
how to become a barista for Starbucks.

Tina is ready to graduate with a checking and savings account, a job, and a home.

She now lives in Maine. Her son, who is a chef, lives down the street from her. Tina loves her job and is designing and building guitar parts.

Dear Marilyn,

I can not Thank you or the house of Sophia enough for the help, encouragement & support you have given Tina.

She is a changed woman and we are so very proud of her accomplishments.

Thanks you for being there for her.

from me to you!

Sincerely,

Tina called me in 2014... She loves the Lord and is attending a local church, has acclimated to her community, and is very happy and joyful.

Two weeks after intake at the House
of Sophia.

After thirty days,
our client is already
working the deli at Vons.

Graduation: A beautiful working mother went home
to her sixteen-year-old daughter.

Deb came to HOS without a home. One evening, her husband, who was also without a home or job, came to the HOS. He demanded that I release his wife, even threatening bodily harm to me if I didn't comply. I informed him that she was in a program and could not be released for at least thirty days. Deb was doing so well at the HOS and was gainfully employed. Eventually, Deb graduated, and we were able to get the couple, and their children settled in an apartment.

Soon thereafter, they moved in with
eighty-year-old Mildred (3rd from the right) and
remained with her until she died.
About one year later, I received this card.

God brings joy
into our lives
In very
special ways...
Like friendships
seeded in His love
To brighten
all our days.

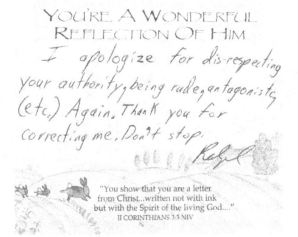

Your friendship is a way God
shows His goodness to me!

YOU'RE A WONDERFUL
REFLECTION OF HIM

I apologize for dis-respecting
your authority, being rude, antagonistic
(etc.) Again, Thank you for
correcting me. Don't stop.

Ralph

"You show that you are a letter
from Christ...written not with ink
but with the Spirit of the living God...."
II CORINTHIANS 3:3 NIV

From Deb's husband, Ralph

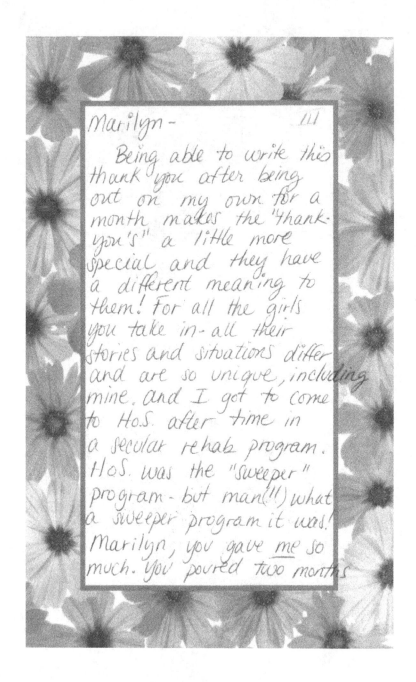

Marilyn —

Being able to write this thank you after being out on my own for a month makes the "thank-you's" a little more special and they have a different meaning to them! For all the girls you take in - all their stories and situations differ and are so unique, including mine. And I got to come to Ho.S. after time in a secular rehab program. Ho.S. was the "sweeper" program - but man(!!) what a sweeper program it was! Marilyn, you gave me so much. You poured two months of your life into me! I can't say that about many people. Not only did you pour yourself into your work, you allowed the Spirit, and Christ to work mightily in that house during my stay. You allowed me to be emptyied, so I could be filled. You allowed me to be weakened so I could be strengthned. You allowed me to seek forgiveness, TRUE forgiveness so I could be forgiven. You allowed me to be accepted by Him so that I could be LOVED!

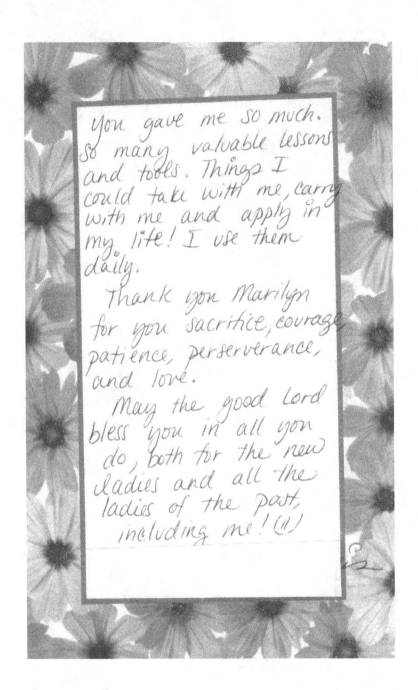

You gave me so much.
So many valuable lessons
and tools. Things I
could take with me, carry
with me and apply in
my life! I use them
daily.

Thank you Marilyn
for you sacrifice, courage,
patience, perserverance,
and love.

May the good Lord
bless you in all you
do, both for the new
ladies and all the
ladies of the past,
including me! (!)

Testimony - Derah

My name is Derah. I'm thirty-five, the mother of two. Last year I was at the end of my rope. Living in complete darkness. I wanted to die every day for a year or two before that. I knew I was going to end it. My doctor put me in Palomar Hospital with a police escort. There I met Valerie, the social worker, and I told her I wanted to die. She had this big smile on her face and said, "Do I have a place for you! Derah, if you trust me, I can get you into the House of Sophia." I was pretty out of it by then. I had swallowed a lot of pills. I said I'd do anything she said. Val asked me to trust her and stay overnight in the mental part of the hospital. That was one of the scariest nights I've ever had.

In the morning, my girlfriend took me to the House of Sophia. That was April 1999. I arrived with my ankles all swollen from alcohol. The first two days was detoxing. They gave me my space, and it was pretty terrible. It was total war going on inside me. I couldn't sleep, and I was shaking very badly. From there, I just knew instantly that I had made the right decision.

I really needed the bible study and the books, and the structure, and the rest. Just the rest. I wanted to go right back to work. But Marilyn put her foot down and told me that my work was to get to know God. I studied constantly, read constantly, went to bible studies had discipling by Terry, Eileen, and Mary. It was incredible. I did a lot of crying. A lot of times, anger came out. After the first month, though, I didn't have so many outbursts. I was in contact with my pastor, too. Marilyn had meetings with pastors and their wives, and they put a whole plan together for me. The House of Sophia helped me look into school and get everything in order with my life. I was totally accountable, which I needed — to be completely guarded and sheltered and find peace and rest. Not so much sleep-rest, but rest in my soul.

I worked a lot around the house. That gave me a lot of nurturing. I had a lot of battles to go through with Marilyn. We learned to resolve conflict. I learned that you could work through issues. I wanted to pick up and run a few times. But I learned we could walk away for a while, pray and come back. I learned to deal with other people when they're going through their problems and difficulties. The discipline was important. Marilyn helped me make a plan for what I wanted to achieve, and we talked about when I was ready to go, and I worked with my pastors on what would be best for me. I had a lot of parenting classes to reestablish how to be a mother.

Question: You changed your goals in life and went through a career change. Can you tell us about that?

I have a spelling problem, and I never thought I could do anything but wait tables or work in bars, as I've done my whole life. But Marilyn helped me go deep and see what I really desired, even if I thought I couldn't do it. I told her I wanted to be in the medical field. She helped me see that I could achieve it through God. I never thought I could even get close. I started first by getting a job as a cargiver. Marilyn and Jose and Valerie helped me fill out applications. They helped me know how to come across and be professional about it. I worked full-time while I was going to school. Forty hours a week, and I was going to school, four days a week. Now, I'm interning at Scripps hospital. I have my first interview today to be hired per diem. I want to go on for more schooling, so I can train to be a lab technician.

Question: What is your hope for the future?

Just to continue day by day by God's grace. I want to move through the medical field, to move up to the lab, so I can support my family in this career. I'm good at it. I love every minute of it.

Question: What kind of grades have you had in school?

Straight A's and B+, which cracked me up. They want to hire me right now. My teacher has given me a recommendation, and I've made my first resume. You never had to make a resume to work in a bar.

Question: Would you recommend to someone else to go to the House of Sophia?

They have to really want it. I knew there were programs, but since I wasn't homeless, I thought I didn't need one.

Question. You were suicidal. Do you have any problem with that now?

Now, I share a house with two other women. We've carried some things over from the House of Sophia to our house. We're very accountable to one another. We don't have cable. We don't date. We would court if God brought the right man. Men aren't allowed in our house unless we're all there, and there's a reason. We have a house meeting every Sunday night. We have house chores. I don't think there's any way, unless we did things in order, the way the House of Sophia does, that we could get along so well.

Question: Anything to add?

Just that I don't know what I would have done if there wasn't somebody out there to help me.

Derah received a scholarship from the same hospital that had earlier admitted her because she was suicidal. She worked in that hospital, having come full circle.

Appendix

Contracts

Priceless contracts finalized over twenty years as needed. Given with permission by attorney Deborah Dewart.

HOUSE OF SOPHIA
DISCIPLESHIP MINISTRY AGREEMENT

In consideration for my admission to the residential program offered by the HOUSE OF SOPHIA, a California **religious** nonprofit corporation, I hereby acknowledge and agree to all of the following terms and conditions:

Goal of Program: The purpose of the House of Sophia's residential discipleship program is to help residents meet the challenges of life in a way that will please and honor the Lord Jesus Christ.

I acknowledge my need for intense discipleship in a residential setting, and accordingly, I willingly and voluntarily associate myself with the House of Sophia. I enter this Christian discipleship program of my own free will. Although I understand that I may dissociate myself from the program at any time, I hereby make a good faith commitment to a residential term of at least _____ months, including my probation period of ____ days.

Biblical Basis for Program: I acknowledge that the House of Sophia is a Christ-centered community that uses prayer, daily Bible studies, work, and spiritual discipleship through staff, peers, and third party mentoring relationships (when available and appropriate). My purpose and intent in joining this residential discipleship ministry is to seek Christ-centered living skills, and to live under the lordship of Jesus Christ and His Word, as taught and modeled within the House of Sophia community.

I understand that any counseling offered by or arranged through House of Sophia is strictly religious in nature, conducted under the authority and leadership of the church. House of Sophia is committed to the belief that God, through His revelation in the Old and New Testaments of the Bible, has provided His people with thorough guidance and instruction for faith and life (II Timothy 3:16-17; II Peter 1:3-4). Any counseling offered by or arranged through this program is based solely on biblical principles. House of Sophia rejects the teachings and methods of modern psychology or psychiatry, whether expressly secular or an attempted integration with the Bible. All counselors affiliated with House of Sophia are <u>not</u> trained or licensed as psychotherapists or mental health professionals, and under California law no such licensing is required. They do not follow

1

112

the methods of such persons, and House of Sophia's policy is to not make referrals to them.

I understand that the House of Sophia may from time to time arrange counseling services during my residency, through the Institute for Biblical Counseling and Discipleship (a ministry of the Bayview Orthodox Presbyterian Church) or through a local Bible-believing church.

I agree that, while residing at the House of Sophia, I will not seek the services of any psychologist, psychotherapist, or similarly trained mental health professional.

Monthly Tuition and Costs: In consideration for the discipleship program to be provided by House of Sophia, I agree to pay the following amounts:

Month #1:	$ _____
Month #2:	$ _____
Month #3:	$ _____
Month #4:	$ _____
Month #5:	$ _____
Month #6:	$ _____

I understand that such payments help the House of Sophia defray the costs of my room and board (including meals), utilities, laundry, and transportation.

In addition, I agree to reimburse the House of Sophia promptly, upon presentation of written documentation, for the cost of long distance telephone calls, supplies, or other similar expenses that are not covered by the monthly fees.

No Employer-Employee Relationship: I understand that one aspect of the residential program is to develop godly work habits and structure. In order to accomplish this goal, I agree that during my residency I will, as I am physically able, work in and around the facilities owned and operated by House of Sophia. I acknowledge that no employer-employee relationship shall exist

2

between the House of Sophia and myself at any time during my residency. I will not be entitled to receive wages, worker's compensation, or any other benefits normally associated with an employment relationship.

I understand that from time to time, typically in the first few weeks of residency, a resident with no outside income or support may receive a gratuity payment to assist with the monthly tuition or a special purchase. I acknowledge that such gratuity payments are in the nature of a gift and shall not be considered "wages" paid in exchange for any services performed by me. I agree that no right to such gratuities is created by my association with House of Sophia. Such payments may be unavailable due to the lack of funds, may vary in amount depending on available funds, and may be withheld whenever, in the sole discretion of the House of Sophia, such action is appropriate for disciplinary reasons or for the well-being or safety of any program resident.

Residence Incidental to Discipleship Association: I understand that the residential living quarters provided to me by House of Sophia are incidental to the discipleship program and may be withdrawn at any time, at the sole discretion of the Executive Director of the House of Sophia, without cause or prior notice to me. No right of tenancy of any kind is created by my association with House of Sophia. I understand that residential accommodations will be terminated (1) upon my successful completion of the program, (2) if I am dismissed from the program, (3) if I fail to meet my financial obligations to House of Sophia, or (4) if I voluntarily dissociate myself from the discipleship community.

Personal Property: I assume all risk of loss in connection with any personal property that I choose to bring with me to the House of Sophia, in additional to any such property that I may later acquire and have in my possession during my residency. The risk I hereby assume includes loss caused by fire, flood, earthquake, theft, natural disaster, spoilage, or any other cause.

I agree that upon termination or suspension of my residency at House of Sophia, whether through voluntary dissociation or dismissal for disciplinary reasons, any personal property that I do not take with me upon leaving the premises shall be deemed

3

abandoned, and therefore subject to immediate or later disposal by the House of Sophia (through sale or distribution to others).

Mail: I understand that I may not use the House of Sophia's address for my personal mail, and that I may not disclose such address to third parties without the express consent of the Executive Director.

I agree to make arrangements regarding my personal mail during my residency, as follows:

(1) I may authorize a family member or friend to receive and handle my mail while I am participating in the program; or

(2) I may arrange to pick up my mail accompanied by a representative of the House of Sophia, with the understanding that it will be opened in the presence of the Executive Director.

Confidentiality: Confidentiality is an important aspect of the House of Sophia discipleship program. I understand that House of Sophia representatives will carefully guard the information I entrust to them to the fullest extent possible. However, I understand that certain limited disclosures will be necessary. Examples include, but are not limited to, the following:

1. My pastor, elders, and/or other church leaders should be actively involved in my discipleship program.

2. The Executive Director may discuss issues related to my progress with the House of Sophia Board of Directors and/or legal counsel for the corporation.

3. Members of my family may need to be involved in my program. I understand that House of Sophia will communicate with me, in advance, as to any such involvement.

4. If I refuse to renounce a particular sin, it may become necessary to seek the assistance of others in the church to encourage repentance and reconciliation (Proverbs 15:22, 24:11; Matthew 18:15-20). In such cases, House of Sophia will reveal only such information as is necessary for these purposes, and only to those persons biblically required to be involved.

4

5. Where a House of Sophia representative is uncertain as to how to address a particular issue, he or she may seek advice from my pastor or another biblical counselor who is familiar with the House of Sophia program.

6. If I threaten harm to another person, it may be necessary to intervene in order to prevent such harm. Such intervention may include physical defense by the person threatened or by a House of Sophia representative, to the extent necessary for protection, or contacting the local police.

7. The law may require disclosure of child abuse, or some other crime, to the appropriate authorities.

Other Professional Advice: If I have significant medical, legal, financial, or other technical questions, I understand that I should seek advice from an independent professional. House of Sophia is not engaged in rendering medical, legal, financial, or similar technical advice. However, House of Sophia will cooperate with other advisors and help me to consider their counsel in the light of scriptural principles.

Medical Treatment: I understand that my body is the temple of God, and that I have a responsibility to care for it and to seek proper medical treatment for all physiological problems. House of Sophia may assist me in responding to such problems in a godly manner, but I understand that such spiritual counsel is not intended to replace the services of a qualified physician where organic problems are present or where medication has been prescribed.

I agree that, prior to entering the residential program, I will execute an "Advance Health Care Directive" and provide a copy to House of Sophia. Such directive will specify my desires in the event of a medical emergency, including family members to be notified, and shall provide authorization for emergency treatment in the event that I am unconscious or otherwise unable to expressly consent.

Drugs, Alcohol, and Medications: I understand that I may be immediately terminated from the House of Sophia program if I am found to be in possession of, or under the slightest influence of, any illegal drugs, alcohol, and/or prescription medications for which I do not have a current prescription in my own name.

5

116

Smoking: I understand that, for the health, safety, and comfort of House of Sophia residents and employees, smoking is not permitted during my residency, whether on or away from the ministry premises. I understand that I may be immediately terminated from the program in the event that I am caught smoking.

Violence: I understand that I may be immediately terminated from the program in the event I threaten or actually cause physical harm to another person during my residency, whether on or outside the House of Sophia premises.

Severability: If any term, provision, covenant or condition of this Agreement is held by a court of competent jurisdiction to be invalid, void, or unenforceable, the remainder of the provisions shall remain in full force and effect and shall in no way be affected, impaired, or invalidated.

Entire Agreement: This Agreement contains the entire agreement between myself and House of Sophia, except as otherwise expressly provided herein. All prior negotiations, agreements, and understandings are superseded. This Agreement may not be amended or revised except by a writing signed by myself and a representative of House of Sophia; provided, however, that I agree to abide by such ordinary rules and policies as may be established from time to time. I acknowledge that I have received and read a copy of the current "Rules and Regulations of House of Sophia," and I agree to abide by such rules as if expressly set forth herein. I understand that these rules may be changed from time to time according to the needs of the program and its current residents, and I agree to abide by any such changes.

Governing Law: This Agreement will be construed and enforced in accordance with the laws of the State of California.

Conflict Resolution - Arbitration: Day to day conflicts are to be resolved in accordance with the "Rules and Regulations of House of Sophia." On rare occasions, more serious conflicts may develop between House of Sophia and a resident. 1 Corinthians 6:1-8 forbids Christians from bringing lawsuits against one another in secular courts of law. In order to ensure that such conflicts are resolved in a biblically faithfully manner, I agree that any dispute between myself and House of Sophia will be settled by mediation and, if necessary, legally binding

6

117

arbitration conducted in accordance with the *Rules of Procedure* of the Institute for Christian Conciliation. (A copy is available on request.) The arbiters will be the elders of _____ Church. If one or more elders of the church is a party to the dispute, then three arbiters will be selected from the elders of churches in the Presbytery of _____ of the _____ Church, with each party to the dispute choosing one arbiter, and the two arbiters then selecting the third. It is expressly understood that, by consenting in advance to such arbitration, I am waiving my right to a trial in the civil courts.

I have read the entire Discipleship Ministry Agreement and agree to be bound by all of the terms and conditions stated therein. My signature below indicates that I enter this residential program of my own free will, without coercion of any kind from any person. I understand that I am free at any time, regardless of reason or cause, to discontinue my discipleship association with House of Sophia and to leave the premises.

Signed_____ Dated_____

Printed Name of Resident_____

ACKNOWLEDGMENT BY HOUSE OF SOPHIA

As an authorized representative of House of Sophia, I agree that the corporation will abide by and honor all of its obligations in connection with this Discipleship Ministry Agreement. Having clarified the principles and policies of the ministry, House of Sophia welcomes the opportunity to minister to this resident in the name of Christ and to be used by Him as He helps her grow in spiritual maturity and prepares her for usefulness in His body.

Signed_____ Dated_____

Printed Name_____ Title_____

7

HOUSE OF SOPHIA
RULES AND REGULATIONS

Personal Belongings

1. Residents may bring one bag of personal belongings, all of which must be consistent with the current list of approved items. There is not adequate storage space for more.

2. If a resident leaves without notice, personal belongings will be stored for thirty (30) days and thereafter donated to charity if the former resident has not arranged for their removal.

3. Residents may not borrow or lend personal belongings to other residents during their stay.

Medications and Other Substances

4. The following must not be used at any time, in any place, during the resident's stay:

* Illegal drugs

* Alcoholic beverages

* Non-prescription drugs, except as approved by staff for temporary use (for example, over-the-counter pain killers or cold remedies)

* Smoking is not allowed during the resident's stay, at any time or in any place. This is a no smoking program.

Any prescription medications will be held by staff and administered as prescribed.

Personal Conduct

5. Verbal and physical abuse will not be tolerated at any time and is grounds for immediate dismissal. Residents must not damage or destroy personal property belonging to others, including the House of Sophia, staff, guests, or other residents. Staff reserves the right to contact the police or others for assistance in order to protect people (staff, other residents, neighbors, guests) and property.

6. Telephone calls must be approved and screened by staff and shall not exceed ten (10) minutes. Use of the phone is a privilege, not a right.

7. Residents may not speak to neighbors (beyond a simple "hello" or "good morning") and may not date during their stay. Residents will keep noise at a reasonable level at all times so as not to disturb others.

119

Schedules

8. **WAKE-UP AND BEDTIME**. Residents are responsible to observe schedules for wake-up, bedtime, and meals.

Wake-up Times:
Monday through Friday	5:30 a.m.
Saturday	8:00 a.m.
Sunday	7:30-8:00 a.m. (in time for church)

Staff will make one pot of coffee for the morning meeting. Residents who fail to wake up on their own and prepare themselves for the meeting will not be allowed coffee.

Evening Bedtimes:
Sunday through Thursday	10:00 p.m.
Friday and Saturday	12:00 midnight

Doors will be locked and lights turned out at these times.

9. **MEALS**. Residents are expected to attend all meals at the scheduled times, unless an absence is pre-arranged due to employment or other approved activities. Three daily meals and one snack will be served. Residents must observe the following:

All meals will be served at the table at scheduled times. No food may be taken into a bedroom.

Residents must eat what is served, unless arrangements have been made in advance due to allergies or other legitimate reasons.

Each morning, staff will schedule responsibilities for cooking and cleaning up for that day.

Residents may not be in the kitchen except to fulfill assigned cooking and/or cleaning responsibilities.

10. **CHORES**. Residents are responsible to perform assigned chores on Saturday morning between 9:00 a.m. and 12:00 noon.

11. **LAUNDRY**. Residents may do two (2) loads of laundry weekly, to be scheduled and supervised. Sheets and towels must be washed once per week.

12. **OFF LIMITS AREAS**. Certain areas are strictly off-limits to residents without prior invitation. Such areas include personal living space for staff and the office area for House of Sophia business.

HOUSE OF SOPHIA
VISITOR'S AGREEMENT

Visitors must sign and agree to the following:

RELIGIOUS NATURE OF PROGRAM

I understand that the House of Sophia is a Christ-centered community that uses prayer, daily Bible studies, work, and spiritual discipleship through staff, peers, and third party mentoring relationships (when available and appropriate).

I understand that the House of Sophia program is strictly religious in nature, conducted under the authority and leadership of the church. House of Sophia is committed to the belief that God, through His Word, has provided sufficient guidance and instruction for faith and life (II Timothy 3:16-17; II Peter 1:3-4). **Any counseling offered by or arranged through this program is based solely on biblical principles.** House of Sophia rejects the teachings and methods of modern psychology. Counselors affiliated with this program are not trained or licensed as psychological counselors and do not hold themselves out as such.

MEDICAL ISSUES

I understand that House of Sophia does not offer medical treatment. Its staff has no medical training and will not undertake responsibility for a person who is seriously ill. I represent that I have no medical condition that would require medical expertise. In the event of an unforeseen life-threatening emergency (for example, a heart attack), House of Sophia will call "911" and then contact the person I designate in this Agreement. In case of other medical problems, my visit will be immediately terminated and House of Sophia will contact my designated person to make arrangements for transportation to my home or doctor.

If I am taking any prescription medication, it is listed below, and I will provide a sufficient supply to be placed in a safe, unlocked place that I may access during my visit. I understand that taking such medication is my sole responsibility.

Medications (if any)_____

1

I designate the following person to be contacted in case the need arises for medical care or treatment:

Name_____

Relationship_____

Phone Number(s)_____

SUPERVISION

I understand that I will not be allowed to remain in the residence alone at any time during my visit. If it is necessary for staff to leave for any purpose, I will either accompany her or my visit will be terminated. I understand that this policy is necessary to protect both the House of Sophia and myself.

SIGNATURES

My signature below indicates that I am visiting this residential program of my own free will, without coercion of any kind from any person. I understand that I am free at any time, regardless of reason or cause, to discontinue my visit and leave the premises.

Signed_____ Dated_____

Printed Name of Visitor _____

ACKNOWLEDGMENT BY HOUSE OF SOPHIA

As an authorized House of Sophia representative, I agree that the corporation will abide by and honor all of its obligations in connection with this Agreement. Having clarified the ministry's principles and policies, we welcome the opportunity to minister to this person in the name of Christ and to be used by Him for her spiritual growth.

Signed_____ Dated_____

Printed Name_____ Title_____

2

In consideration for my admission to the day program offered by the House of Sophia, a California **religious** nonprofit corporation, I hereby acknowledge and agree to all of the following terms and conditions:

Goal of Program: The purpose of the House of Sophia's discipleship program is to help participants meet the challenges of life in a way that will please and honor the Lord Jesus Christ.

I acknowledge my need for intense discipleship, and accordingly, I willingly and voluntarily associate myself with the House of Sophia. I enter this Christian discipleship program of my own free will. Although I understand that I may dissociate myself from the program at any time, I hereby make a good faith commitment to the program for a term of at least _____ months, including my probation period of _____ days.

Biblical Basis for Program: I acknowledge that the House of Sophia is a Christ-centered program that uses prayer, daily Bible studies, work, and spiritual discipleship through staff, peers, and third party mentoring relationships (when available and appropriate). My purpose and intent in joining this discipleship ministry is to seek Christ-centered living skills, and to live under the lordship of Jesus Christ and His Word, as taught and modeled within the House of Sophia community.

I understand that any counseling offered by or arranged through House of Sophia is strictly religious in nature, conducted under the authority and leadership of the church. House of Sophia is committed to the belief that God, through His revelation in the Old and New Testaments of the Bible, has provided His people with thorough guidance and instruction for faith and life (2 Timothy 3:16-17; 2 Peter 1:3-4). Any counseling offered by or arranged through this program is based solely on biblical principles. House of Sophia rejects the teachings and methods of modern psychology or psychiatry, whether expressly secular or an attempted integration with the Bible. All counselors affiliated with House of Sophia are not trained or licensed as psychotherapists or mental health professionals, and under California law no such licensing is required. They do not follow

1

the methods of such persons, and House of Sophia's policy is to not make referrals to them.

I understand that the House of Sophia may from time to time arrange counseling services for me, through House of Sophia personnel, the Institute for Biblical Counseling and Discipleship (a ministry of the Bayview Orthodox Presbyterian Church) or a local Bible-believing church, such as the North City Presbyterian (PCA) Church in Poway, CA.

I agree that, while participating in the House of Sophia day program, I will not seek the services of any psychologist, psychotherapist, or similarly trained mental health professional.

Submission to Authority at the House of Sophia:
Human beings are created in the image of God (Genesis 1:26-27) but have fallen into sin (Genesis 3:1-24, 6:5, 8:21; Psalm 51:5; Jeremiah 17:9; Romans 3:9-23) and therefore have a natural inclination to rebel against authority and authority figures. However, participants in the House of Sophia program are expected to follow all directions given by the program director or other authorized persons. Submission to authority is a biblical principle. It is not trust in or obedience to a human person, but rather trust in God and obedience to His Word. Participants are expected to obey and follow directions given by the program director, even where it is undesirable or uncomfortable. This is obedience to godly authority, based on trust in God, who established that authority:

> "Let every person be subject to the governing authorities. For there is no authority except from God and those that exist have been instituted by God. Therefore, whoever resists the authorities resists what God has appointed.... For he is God's servant for your good."

Romans 13:1-2, 4

In addition to submitting to the authority of House of Sophia representatives, I agree to abide by the House of Sophia "Rules and Regulations."

Church Premises: I understand that a substantial portion of the House of Sophia day program is conducted on the premises of North City Presbyterian (PCA) Church, located in Poway, CA. The

2

124

NCPC Church Board has graciously consented to the use of its premises for this discipleship program and offers its prayerful support, blessing, and counsel. However, I understand that House of Sophia is a separate corporation, governed by a separate Board of Directors, and that House of Sophia is solely responsible for the financing and conduct of the program.

Monthly Tuition and Costs: In consideration for the discipleship program to be provided by House of Sophia, I agree to pay the monthly charge of $400.00 per month.

I understand that such payments help the House of Sophia defray the costs of operating the program.

In addition, I agree to reimburse the House of Sophia promptly, upon presentation of written documentation, for the cost of expenses incurred on my behalf that are not covered by the monthly fee.

> **Refund Policy**. **There will be no refunds of any tuition payments, unless the Board of Directors shall agree that a refund is appropriate under the circumstances.**

Tax Deductibility. I understand that the Internal Revenue Service does not allow a charitable contribution deduction where goods and/or services are received in exchange for payments to a tax-exempt organization. Therefore, the payments required for my day program at House of Sophia are not tax deductible.

However, House of Sophia is a Christian ministry that is continually in need of contributions (both cash and donations in kind) in order to survive and to continue to offer its unique biblical program. House of Sophia has established its tax-exempt status with the Internal Revenue Service and California Franchise Tax Board, and it qualifies to receive tax-deductible contributions. If a participant is able to contribute beyond the required program fees, the excess will be tax-deductible. All donations are greatly appreciated and will help House of Sophia to continue providing this ministry.

No Employer-Employee Relationship: I acknowledge that no employer-employee relationship shall exist between the House of Sophia and myself at any time during my participation in the day program. I will not be entitled to receive wages, worker's

3

compensation, or any other benefits normally associated with an employment relationship.

Personal Property: I assume all risk of loss in connection with any personal property that I choose to bring with me to the House of Sophia day program. The risk I hereby assume includes loss caused by fire, flood, earthquake, theft, natural disaster, spoilage, or any other cause.

I agree that upon termination or suspension of my participation in the House of Sophia day program, whether through voluntary dissociation or dismissal for disciplinary reasons, any personal property that I do not take with me upon leaving the premises shall be deemed abandoned, and therefore subject to immediate or later disposal by the House of Sophia (through sale or distribution to others).

Confidentiality: Confidentiality is an important aspect of the House of Sophia discipleship program. I understand that House of Sophia representatives will carefully guard the information I entrust to them to the fullest extent possible. However, I understand that certain limited disclosures will be necessary. Examples include, but are not limited to, the following:

1. My pastor, elders, and/or other church leaders should be actively involved in my discipleship program.

2. The Executive Director may discuss issues related to my progress with the House of Sophia Board of Directors and/or legal counsel for the corporation.

3. Members of my family may need to be involved in my program. I understand that House of Sophia will communicate with me, in advance, as to any such involvement.

4. If I refuse to renounce a particular sin, it may be necessary to seek the assistance of others in the church to encourage repentance and reconciliation (Proverbs 15:22, 24:11; Matthew 18:15-20: Galatians 6:1-2). In such cases, House of Sophia will reveal only such information as is necessary for these purposes, and only to those persons biblically required to be involved.

4

5. Where a House of Sophia representative is uncertain as to how to address a particular issue, he or she may seek advice from my pastor or another biblical counselor who is familiar with the House of Sophia program.

6. If I threaten harm to another person, it may be necessary to intervene in order to prevent such harm. Such intervention may include physical defense by the person threatened or by a House of Sophia representative, to the extent necessary for protection, or contacting the local police.

7. The law may require disclosure of child abuse, or some other crime, to the appropriate authorities.

Other Professional Advice: If I have significant medical, legal, financial, or other technical issues, I understand that I should seek advice from an independent professional. House of Sophia is not engaged in rendering medical, legal, financial, or similar technical advice. However, House of Sophia will cooperate with other advisors and help me to consider their counsel in the light of scriptural principles.

Medical Treatment: I understand that my body is the temple of God, and I have a responsibility to care for it and seek proper medical treatment for all physiological problems. House of Sophia may assist me in responding to such problems in a godly manner, but I understand that such spiritual counsel is not intended to replace the services of a qualified physician where organic problems are present or where medication has been prescribed.

I agree that, prior to entering the day program, I will execute an "Advance Health Care Directive" and provide a copy to House of Sophia. Such directive will specify my desires in the event of a medical emergency, including family members to be notified, and shall provide authorization for emergency treatment in the event that I am unconscious or otherwise unable to expressly consent.

Drugs, Alcohol, and Medications: I understand that I may be immediately terminated from the House of Sophia program if I am found to be in possession of, or under the slightest influence of, any illegal drugs, alcohol, and/or prescription medications for which I do not have a current prescription in my own name.

5

Smoking: I understand that, for the health, safety, and comfort of House of Sophia participants and personnel, smoking is not permitted during my participation in the program, whether on or away from the ministry premises. I understand that I may be immediately terminated from the program in the event that I am caught smoking.

Violence: I understand that I may be immediately terminated from the program in the event I threaten or actually cause physical harm to another person during my participation in the program, whether on or outside the premises where the House of Sophia program is conducted.

Permission for Use of Picture and First Name: From time to time, House of Sophia uses pictures and first names of women who have participated in the program, in order to inform others and inspire future participants to walk with the Lord, taking the first step down the road to restoration. Participants may either grant permission, or decline, by initialing the following:

	YES	NO
You may use my picture to promote the House of Sophia program:	_____	_____
You may use my first name to promote the House of Sophia program	_____	_____
Please contact me before you use my picture or name:	_____	

Severability: If any term, provision, covenant or condition of this Agreement is held by a court of competent jurisdiction to be invalid, void, or unenforceable, the remainder of the provisions shall remain in full force and effect and shall in no way be affected, impaired, or invalidated.

Entire Agreement: This Agreement contains the entire agreement between myself and House of Sophia, except as otherwise expressly set forth herein. All prior negotiations, agreements, and understandings are superseded. This Agreement may not be amended or revised except by a writing signed by myself and a representative of House of Sophia; provided, however, that I agree to abide by such ordinary rules and policies as may be established

6

128

from time to time. I acknowledge that I have received and read a copy of the current "Rules and Regulations of House of Sophia," and I agree to abide by such rules as if expressly set forth herein. I understand that these rules may be changed from time to time according to the needs of the program and its current participants, and I agree to abide by any such changes.

Governing Law: This Agreement will be construed and enforced in accordance with the laws of the State of California.

Conflict Resolution - Arbitration: Day to day conflicts will be resolved in accordance with the "Rules and Regulations of House of Sophia." On rare occasions, more serious conflicts may develop between House of Sophia and a program participant. 1 Corinthians 6:1-8 forbids Christians from bringing lawsuits against one another in secular courts of law. In order to ensure that such conflicts are resolved in a biblically faithfully manner, I agree that any dispute between myself and House of Sophia will be settled by mediation and, if necessary, legally binding arbitration conducted in accordance with the *Rules of Procedure* of the Institute for Christian Conciliation. (A copy is available on request.) The arbiters will be the elders of North City Presbyterian (PCA) Church. If one or more elders of the church is a party to the dispute, then three arbiters will be selected from the elders of churches in the Presbytery of Presbyterian Church in America (PCA), with each party to the dispute choosing one arbiter, and the two arbiters then selecting the third. It is expressly understood that, by consenting in advance to such arbitration, I am waiving my right to a trial in the civil courts.

//
//
//
//
//
//
//
//
//
//
//
//
//
//
//

HOUSE OF SOPHIA
DISCIPLESHIP MINISTRY AGREEMENT
DAY PROGRAM

SIGNATURE OF MINISTRY PARTICIPANT

I have read the entire Discipleship Ministry Agreement and agree to be bound by all of the terms and conditions stated therein. My signature below indicates that I enter this day program of my own free will, without coercion of any kind from any person. I understand that I am free at any time, regardless of reason or cause, to discontinue my discipleship association with House of Sophia and to leave the premises.

Signed_____ Dated_____

Printed Name of Participant_____

ACKNOWLEDGMENT BY HOUSE OF SOPHIA

As an authorized representative of House of Sophia, I agree that the corporation will abide by and honor all of its obligations in connection with this Discipleship Ministry Agreement. Having clarified the principles and policies of the ministry, House of Sophia welcomes the opportunity to minister to this person in the name of Christ and to be used by Him as He helps her grow in spiritual maturity and prepares her for usefulness in His body.

Signed_____ Dated_____

Printed Name_____ Title_____

8

130

About the Author

About me — the girl on the cover... I've lived a tumultuous childhood and a very BIG life. I graduated from a prestigious seminary and had twenty years of ministry as the founder, director of the House of Sophia, which housed over one hundred women in a residential program. I was able to take six trips as a team leader to Africa, completing a 7,000 square foot building project used for training pastors, feeding people, food distributions, and more. I also had a food ministry, feeding over 700 people per month, and all are ongoing. Helping, helping, and forever helping people in need! The most golden nugget I have is not to work for my salvation. It is leaning on the Lord to work out my salvation daily and to praise Him every day for allowing me to work for the Kingdom. My hope in penning this book is to guide weary leaders working in a world of craziness. Bottom line. There is a God who has a purpose for our journey, and we are pilgrims heading home. Thank you, Lord. Use this work for your Kingdom.

My publisher, Janet Sierzant, with a nudge, a push, and frequent encouragement, is responsible for this book coming to complete fruition. Without her extensive expertise, I would never have accomplished the vision of my friends who joined me on this incredible journey. Those friends urged me to write this "how-to" book that would forge the way for others so that they would have a blueprint for duplicating our Christian residential program. They would join me with a hearty appreciation for Janet's perseverance.

La Maison Publishing, Inc.
Vero Beach, Florida
The Hibiscus City

Maison

9 781970 153262